Educational Communication
In A Revolutionary Age

EDGAR DALE

Educational Communication
In A Revolutionary Age

Compiled by - I. Keith Tyler
Professor of Education

and

Catharine M. Williams
Associate Professor
of Education

The Ohio State University

Charles A. Jones Publishing Company
Worthington, Ohio

✓

1 2 3 4 5 6 7 8 9 10 / 76 75 74 73 72

Library of Congress Catalog Card Number: 72-92633
International Standard Book Number: 0-8396-0033-x

Printed in the United States of America

FOREWORD

It is almost trite to say that we live in a critical and tumultuous time. But in this very period which requires thoughtful examination, we find ourselves inordinately busy. And most of us carry heavy responsibilities.

Nevertheless, we should pause, now and again, to re-examine our day-to-day pursuits in the perspective of perennial crisis, for we truly live in an age of continuing revolution. This volume should provide substance and occasion for such reappraisal.

Brought together here is a series of papers prepared as tributes to Edgar Dale by outstanding figures in the field in which he labored—educational communications. The event which motivated these reflective writings was the retirement of Professor Dale during the Centennial Year of The Ohio State University. It was a time for rejoicing in past achievements and making bold resolutions for the future. And since Edgar Dale is, above all else, an educator, it was a time to assess the educational establishment, its past, present and future. Indeed, it was particularly appropriate to address the future toward which the University enterprise is pointed and to which most of Dr. Dale's efforts have been and are directed. Only such forward looking statements could be expected to have meaningful consequences in the years ahead.

The principal papers represent the varied arenas of Edgar Dale's lifelong endeavors. They are the thoughtful work of distinguished scholars in these fields. Occasionally a paper is accompanied by the critical comments of other well-qualified academics in order to illuminate or challenge an expressed viewpoint.

Increasingly, in the strife of confrontation and conflict,

whether political, social, economic or personal, the need for fundamental understanding becomes strikingly apparent. The times cry out for continuous and meaningful communication. This is no less true in education with its basic dependence upon interaction between learner and teacher. Clearly, then, educational communications was most aptly an appropriate focus for this volume. Additionally, it requires no great prescience to recognize that the years ahead, like those in which we now live, will continue the age of revolution. And by revolution is meant not only rapid change and innovation but also an alteration of character resulting in new forms and functions. This is increasingly characteristic of our times and of the areas under scrutiny in these articles. Hence the theme of this publication: Educational Communication in a Revolutionary Age.

Almost without exception all who were asked to participate in this collective enterprise accepted, in itself a high tribute to Edgar Dale. Financial support was provided not only by the University Centennial Committee but also by organizations with which Professor Dale has worked: American Educational Publications, The Field Enterprises Educational Corporation, International Business Machines Corporation, and The Payne Fund.

The central purpose of this volume, then, is to stimulate the reader to reflect upon what the future may bring in the several fields in which Edgar Dale toiled throughout his professional life. Hopefully each of us may gain insights that will lead to more fruitful and meaningful efforts in the baffling and chaotic times that lie ahead.

I. KEITH TYLER
Professor of Education
The Ohio State University

PROFILE OF EDGAR DALE

At the time of his retirement from Ohio State University, Edgar Dale was a professor in the Faculty of Curriculum and Foundations, College of Education, and an internationally recognized authority in the field of educational communications.

A native of Minnesota, he received both the bachelor's and master's degrees from the University of North Dakota and his doctor of philosophy degree from the University of Chicago. In November 1958, he was awarded the honorary degree of doctor of humanities from the University of North Dakota.

Dr. Dale began his teaching career in 1918 in a rural school in North Dakota. His interest in films as an educational medium took him to Rochester, N. Y., in 1928 as a member of the editorial staff of Eastman Teaching Films. He joined the Ohio State University faculty in 1929 as a research associate in the former Bureau of Educational Research. He became a professor of education in 1939.

During World War II he was head of the coordination division of the Bureau of Motion Pictures, Office of War Information. He served as consultant for the War Department in producing instructional training films and worked with the first motion picture unit in Hollywood as technical consultant for the film *Instructional Methods in the Army Air Forces.*

In 1948 Dr. Dale served as a member of the Commission on Technical Needs in Press, Film, and Radio which met in Paris. He was asked to return to the 1949 meeting of this commission as its chairman.

Dr. Dale is the author of a number of books including *How to Appreciate Motion Pictures* (1935), *Teaching with Motion Pictures* (1937), *How to Read a Newspaper* (1941), *Audio-Visual Methods in Teaching* (first published in 1946, now in its third edition and translated into Spanish, Japanese, and Urdu), *Can You Give the Public What It Wants?* (1967), and *Techniques of Teaching Vocabulary* (1971), co-authored with Joseph O'Rourke.

Throughout his career, Dr. Dale has worked on ways of improving the simplicity and clarity of books, pamphlets and newspapers and has developed a readability formula for determining grade levels of reading materials. He is the author of three readers used in the literacy program of the armed forces and was chairman of the committee that produced the book *Mass Media and Education.*

For the past 36 years, Dr. Dale was editor of "The News Letter," a monthly publication dealing with developments in film, radio and press pertinent to education.

He served four years as the Educational Film Library Association's representative to the U. S. National Commission for UNESCO, and has also been an educational consultant to the National Tuberculosis Association, the Community Chest and Councils, Inc., and the Fund for Adult Education, established by the Ford Foundation.

Edgar Dale was an early president of the Department of Audio-Visual Instruction, National Education Association. He has been a member of the Board of Directors of the National Society for the Study of Education and a member of the Educational Policies Commission. He serves on the Advisory Board of the World Book Encyclopedia and the board of directors of the National Association for Better Broadcasting.

In 1961 Dr. Dale became the first recipient of the Educational Film Library Association's annual award which was presented to him for "distinguished service in the audio-visual field." He was one of five Ohio State University faculty members who received Alumni Awards for Distinguished Teaching in 1963. In 1968 he was selected by the Society of Motion Picture and Television Engineers to receive the Eastman Kodak Gold Medal Award. In 1972, he received a distinguished service award from the Association for Educational Communications and Technology.

Since retirement Dr. Dale has continued his activities. In 1971 he participated in a conference on instructional technology in Australia. He also served as a consultant for six weeks in Piracicaba, Brazil at the Escola Superior de Agricultura. In 1972 a monograph was published by Phi Delta Kappa titled, *Building A Learning Environment*. During the fall of 1972 he conducted a two-week seminar on communication and technology at ILCE (Latin American Institute for Educational Communication) in Mexico City.

CONTENTS

INTRODUCTION

Minds at Large in an Age of Revolution

Robert W. Wagner

Human crisis is characterized by increasing concentration of all cognitive processes and all channels of communication on the immediate calamity, generally accompanied by a corresponding decrease in the perception of broader issues and goals not directly related to the specific problem at hand. The authors of this book, however, manage to deal with the current revolutionary issues in education without losing sight of evolutionary values and long-range effects of media and methods on teacher and learner.

In the following papers, references to "the failures of education," "the impotence of the school," "the need for sweeping change," the existence of a "systems break," and "incipient civil war," are predictable products of a full-blown revolution which, though it began long before, reached a dramatic peak in the Spring of 1970,

Robert W. Wagner is chairman of the Department of Photography and Cinema, The Ohio State University.

1

and continues, in various forms, today.

In May of that year, the writers of this book were gathered with others in a conference to honor the retirement of Dr. Edgar Dale from The Ohio State University, where he had served 41 years of his long and distinguished career. It was also a part of the Centennial celebration of that university.

These are the thoughts of minds-at-large, speaking out of professional wisdom and experience which puts the crisis in education in perspective. Their observations are made, not in a state of panic, but in a mood of concern tempered by a deep sense of mutual confidence and critical sharing which is the necessary prerequisite for both learning and communicating.

Revolution, distinguished from confusion, is defined as "the process of unmasking our social institutions and their instrumentalities . . . the unmasking of some of our educational myths." The school as "a sorting system" is distinguished from the school as "a teaching system." Evaluation in the educational world of today is recognized as being as different as Newtonian mechanics is different from Einsteinian mechanics in the physical world, and is seen by one writer as "something that we all have to do." Continual, knowledgeable change, "productive disequilibrium," is identified as a necessary condition for educational renewal.

The subject of educational communication is explored, and the need for "a common rhetoric" is examined. The role of media is seen as one of "revelation," in "the direction of increased social orientation, art and humanities, and social control of technology." At least one author believes that the future "will include extensive use of computer technology, flexible scheduling, and programmed instruction as part of a growing electronic network feeding into homes, schools,

2

and offices." Another asks: "In the revelation of discrete and different phenomena are camera and film serving only as a window from one discipline to another? Or is there some deeper current flowing, with the camera and the film the indispensable interpreter?"

The collected talents and experiences reflected in this volume include the names of pioneers and leaders in the field of educational communication who have devoted a lifetime of thought and experimentation to how media, from book to computer, may promote teaching and learning, provide for productive disequilibrium, improve the common rhetoric, and expand opportunities for excellence in education for all people in all parts of the world. The media of communication contribute to the concentration of attention on human calamity, social crisis, and the revolution in education, but they are also spark-gaps, bridging "systems breaks," providing a means of revelation in time of revolution.

In the pages that follow, the authors explore the field of educational communication in terms of values which rise above the tempest of the times. "The great revolution in education," concludes the man who wrote one of the first significant books on audiovisual methods in teaching, "will not come through technology, although it may be greatly aided by it. It will come as we shift the role of both the teacher and the student."

Another pioneer in the field says: "I don't think that any of our promising technologies of instruction is going to make very much difference in performance levels of our school system until we learn to respect human beings simply because they are human, until we set higher levels of expectation, free of class, color, and dialect, and until we communicate this human respect and higher expectation to our students." As we combine this humanistic dimension with those of technology, testing, curriculum development, and evaluation we may tend to agree with another distinguished educator who writes: "Now we are better able to talk about the probability of educating an individual in a particular school situation."

The sudden demotion and promotion of individuals and groups is a basic condition of revolution, but Emerson, writing in 1874, a period of relative stability, noted that all authority figures, including educators, are eventually revealed as common clay. "For a time," he wrote, "our teachers serve us personally, as meters or milestones of progress. Once they were angels of knowledge, and their figures touched the sky. Then we drew near, saw their means, culture, and limits, and they yielded their place to other geniuses. Happy, if a few names remain so high, that we have not been able to read them nearer, and age and comparison have not robbed them of a ray."

Happily, this volume includes authors and educators who see beyond the calamities of their time, are possessed of a ballast of wisdom with which to set a course in time of revolution, and whose names, as a consequence, remain so high that age and comparison will not rob them of a ray.

Their clear message is not one of defeat, but of massive action. We must, as one of them put it, "reconceive the goals of education, reconceive the nature of the students we face, reconceive the nature of knowledge, and reconceive ourselves."

Educational Communication in a Revolutionary Age

Charles F. Hoban

In considering revolution and defining it as a process, the thinking of my colleague, Bob Scholte, is insightful and revealing. To oversimplify, he considers revolution as the radicalizing process of unmasking our social institutions and their instrumentalities.

This concept of revolution as an unmasking process carries with it a strong mythic element. A mythic domain is central to any fruitful consideration of communication in education in a revolutionary age; i.e., the contemporary situation. Painful as it may be, we must face up to the unmasking of at least some of our educational myths. (The term "myth" is used to embrace both myth and folklore, thereby eliminating distractions which serve no useful purpose on this occasion.)

In any myth there are at least three elements: (1) events are dramatized, generally in varying versions; (2) the

Charles F. Hoban is a professor in the Annenberg School of Communication, University of Pennsylvania.

events dramatized are generally believed to be true; and, (3) they are relevant to the present; i.e., they have the attribute of what Lynn White, Jr., calls "eternal time."[1]

Unmasking Myths

Let us take two major mythic themes that have dominated the folklore. The one is that education in America is universal; i.e., not limited to an elite—intellectual, social, or otherwise—but embracing all regardless of caste or class. The second theme is related to the first but has an independent existence. It is that in America there is equality of educational opportunity.

The unmasking process of institutionalized education has long since begun. At the hands of John Holt,[2] Edgar Z. Friedenberg,[3] and others of their critical cult, the process of unmasking has become alarming in its overtones of nihilism.

A more moderate observer of the schools, Philip Jackson, the great protector of things-as-they-are-in-the-classroom, likens the social organization of the school to nothing less than a prison.[4] Professor Jackson is a highly perceptive analyst of the social processes of schooling. He is pessimistic toward educational and clinical psychology as operationally applicable to the classroom. He is a tireless enemy of "the engineering approach to teaching." Coming from such a person, the unmasking of the school as a social institution within the same class as the prison represents an extreme form of radicalization on the part of the intellectual elite of the great silent majority.

In our urban heartlands we find the shocking reality of school systems, acclaimed for their innovativeness, actually perpetuating a dismal record of failure to teach a large percentage of their pupils to read and calculate at an acceptable level of functional competence. The prudent sense of ordering the priorities of educational innovation seems to have been lost in the administrative excitement of galloping off in a series of highly publicized "experiments," many of which have little to do with developing one of the most basic of our skills in communication—reading.

When it is suggested that massive attack be made to correct the failures of the schools to prepare students for life in a literate society; i.e., to develop reading skills, the power elite of these school systems somewhat reluctantly admits to the need, but hedges with the admonishment that it will cost more money, that it will require an evaluation program, technical staffing, and the like, all of which should be there in the first place.

The reluctance of professional educators and boards of education to face the ugly facts of institutional underachievement, and to reorder educational priorities accordingly, has led to a broad-based public state of serious doubt and distrust of the American school system. It is being said that professional educators are not competent to perform the tasks of education, that the responsibility for educational planning, management, and administration must be given to others.

The process of unmasking the institution of formal education is approaching an advanced stage of radicalization, and belief in the actuality of universal education and equality of educational opportunity has eroded dangerously.

Dysfunctional Unmasking

This situation has been complicated by two recently published studies by highly reputable scholars in

7

sociology and psychology. One is James S. Coleman's 737-page report of his study of *Equality of Educational Opportunity*.[5] The other is Arthur R. Jensen's 123-page article, "How Much Can We Boost IQ and Scholastic Achievement?"[6]

In their implications, both the Coleman and the Jensen studies are conceptual disasters. Both unmask the wrong institution—in the one case, the family (Coleman), and in the other, race (Jensen). Consequently, both leave the school bland, blameless, helpless, and hopeless. (I am indebted to Basil Bernstein for this insight, as will become evident later in this discussion.)

An essential message of the Coleman report is that "differences between schools account for only a small fraction of differences in pupil achievement." Academic achievement, instead, is strongly related to the family; i.e., to what Coleman categorizes as subjective and objective conditions of the home.

There is, of course, more to the Coleman report than this. A flood of critical controversy has developed since the report was made public. Much of this controversy has centered on statistical aspects of the report *but the more cogent criticism focuses on the transfer of responsibility for poor academic achievement from the school to the family.*

To appreciate the social importance and functions of the family in our contemporary setting, I quote from the historian John Demos:

> Broadly speaking, the history of the family in America has been a history of contraction and withdrawal; its central theme is the gradual surrender to other institutions of functions that once lay very much within the realm of family responsibility.

As to our own times, Demos concludes that:

> The family is important not so much as the foundation
> of an ideal social order, but as the foil to an actual
> state of social disorder. It forms a bulwark against
> the outside world—destroy it (the family) and
> anarchy reigns everywhere. It forms, too, a bulwark
> against anxieties of the deepest and most personal
> kind. For we find in the family, as nowhere else in
> our "open society," an indispensable type of
> protection against the sense of utter isolation and
> helplessness.[7]

If there were only a modicum of truth in the strident
critical literature on education in America, or in the
description of the school as prisonlike, then it is quite
plausible to say that lower socioeconomic status
frequently demands family defense against the
onslaught on children and youth at the hands of our
class-oriented school systems.

It is significant that Eleanor Leacock concludes, from
her study of teacher orientation to caste and class in
urban schools, that (some of the academic performance
attributed by Coleman to socioeconomic factors)
"seemed sufficiently accounted for by the children's
school experience itself."[8]

The Jensen report argues two additional propositions.
The one is that biological inheritance, or what Jensen
calls "heritability," operates in setting the limits of the
IQ; i.e., intelligence narrowly defined. (In passing, I
remember vividly Wilhelm Stern's comment made at
Duke University in the middle 1930's to the effect that
had he realized the extraordinary abuse of the IQ in this
country, he would never have invented the construct.)
Most of us who undertook our graduate studies in the
1930's thought this matter had long since been settled.
We believed it to be the sense of the meeting that what we

call "intelligence" is not a genetic-free human attribute.

The second proposition is more controversial. It rests essentially on the argument that in the Negro race the distribution of "intelligence" is lower in the average and smaller in variance than that of other racial groupings. This is a statistical generalization. As a generalization it is subject to the human propensity to transform generalizations into universals. All universals are applicable to all specific cases and aggregates. In other words, by employing statistical modes of thought, Jensen has painted himself into a conceptual corner, his own precautionary comments to the contrary.

If we employ Jensen's paradigm in dealing with situational actualities of race and IQ, we must conclude that a news note included by Edgar Dale in *The News Letter* of February 1970 is probably a mistake, because what it reports is highly improbable statistically. The news note states that the average IQ of sixth-grade students attending one of the Los Angeles elementary schools exceeded that in all other 435 elementary schools in the district, including high-achieving predominantly white ones. In this particular school, ninety per cent of the students are black. The average IQ of these sixth-graders is 115.

Jensen's first victim, ironically, is himself. The opening sentence of his report is: "Compensatory education has been tried and it apparently has failed." This indicting assertion is made without convincing evidence of fair trial and thus is erroneous in its conclusion.

Probably the most insightful and among the best informed discussions of the conceptual tragedy involved in Jensen's opening sentence comes from Professor Basil Bernstein of the University of London's Institute of Education. In a recent paper Bernstein makes the following comments:

. . . I find the term "compensatory education" a curious one for a number of reasons. I do not understand how we can talk about offering compensatory education to children who, in the first place, have not been offered an adequate educational environment . . .

The concept "compensatory education" serves to direct attention away from the internal organization and the educational context of the school, and focus our attention upon the families and children. The concept "compensatory education" implies that something is lacking in the family and so in the child. As a result the children are unable to benefit from schools. It follows then that the school has to "compensate" for the something which is missing in the family and the children become little deficit systems. If only the parents were interested in the goodies we offer; if only they were like middle class parents, then we could do our job. Once the problem is seen even implicitly in this way, then it becomes appropriate to coin the terms "cultural deprivation," "linguistic deprivation," etc., etc. And then these labels do their own sad work.[9]

Indeed they do.

It is, or so I hope, apparent by now that if we are to avoid disastrous consequences to our schools, our revolution must unmask the implications of reports of some of our most reputable and articulate scholars within the educational profession. Let there be no mistake about it: time is rapidly running out. We must, as I have attempted to do in a small way, hunt down the hunters who are shooting the sheep instead of the wolf.

Communication Principles

Despite the fact that a major activity in schooling is communication, educators in general have shown little interest in serious study of the communication processes. Recently, there has been some study of classroom communication on the verbal level,[10] and some attention has been given to the role of technology in education,[11,12] but little attention has been given to the systematic study of communication in education.

We can begin this necessary task by regarding the ideal or hoped-for end-product of human communication as shared meanings between people. We can then also say it is generally accepted among scholars who have studied the processes of communication from any of several points of view that this transfer is accomplished by the use of symbols.

Having said that, it is also necessary to remark that in education we have tended to narrow the spectrum of symbol systems to (1) the verbal, and (2) the mathematical. We might add the pictorial, but the pictorial symbol system has not been codified, nor has anyone yet succeeded in generating a formal grammar, syntax, or rhetoric of pictorial communication. This, however, may be only an academic dilemma, unrelated to the effectiveness of pictorial communication.

As a practical matter, we can now proceed to four elementary propositions about communication:

1) Everything in our environment has the potential of becoming symbolic, and thus of eliciting meanings among exposed human beings. This proposition expands the repertoire of sources, symbol systems, and scope of educational communication. Without it, educational communication is likely to continue to be viewed in narrowly conventional and over-intellectualistic terms, and we will continue to blind ourselves to the messages of *administrative* procedures, of the fences, chains and locks around our schools, and of our non-verbal behavior.

2) Big technologies, such as television, computerization, and auto-instruction, are suspect by students and teachers alike as dehumanizing because *they are depersonalizing* and because *they run contrary to the emerging social value structure.* I have found this to be so in my own research studies,[13] and Everett Rogers, an international authority on the diffusion of innovation, has observed it at first-hand. Lest I be buried in an avalanche of protest, I hurry to say that I am aware of necessary qualifications and exceptions to the universality of this proposition.

3) The content of any communication is, in the words of my colleague and dean, George Gerbner, "The sum total of warranted inferences that can be made about relationships involved in the communication event."[14] Gerbner's argument is complex, and we need not go into its complexities here. Instead, we need to note that message content lies in *inferences,* and that these inferences concern *relationships* involved in *any informational exchange transaction.* In effect, then, the content of communication is controlled by the receiver as well as by the source, perhaps even more so. This principle of communication is powerful when applied to the experiential curriculum of the school[15] and to the process of communication in education, especially in the context of the first two principles above and the fourth to follow.

4) To a greater extent than generally realized or acknowledged, communication transactions occur in small increments, cumulatively, implicitly, and at the unconscious level. This principle lies at the heart of what Jackson calls "the hidden

curriculum."[16] Contradiction or reversal of this principle lies at the heart of attempts to behavioralize curriculum objectives. If we admit (a) that education is a socializing process, and (b) that the socialization process proceeds at least in part as set forth in the principles of communication we are discussing, then a serious question arises about the imperative that educational objectives be stated and student achievement measured in explicit behavioral performance terms. The question is whether those who insist that teachers must know explicitly what they are trying to accomplish also know explicitly what they themselves are trying to accomplish.

I applaud enthusiasm for conscious awareness of the objectives of teaching, but the dogmatism and extreme emphasis on overt behavior by the advocates make me a little uneasy. I am concerned about the *experiential curriculum* that may be hidden in their structural techniques. Rather than amplify these four principles of communication, I will try to interweave them into a discussion of directions of what I consider to be imperatives of change in the patterns of thinking about communication in education.

Heuristics

Within the formal institution of the school itself, I see five such directions coming to the fore:

1) Increasing recognition of the role of expectation in student growth, development, and performance.

2) Increasing remoteness of control of classroom communication from the teacher in the classroom to some anonymous tutor who plans each detail of content, sequence, required and optional task specification, criteria setting, and testing.

3) A movement away from public communication, with the teacher talking to students in the presence and hearing of all other students in the class, to more private communication between teacher and student on a one-to-one basis.

4) Recognition, however dim, that the media indeed are messages that influence response patterns of students (and adults).

5) The demand that value priorities be reordered to correspond more closely to those of the students and to the needs of society at large.

Expectations. It is unlikely that many of us are unaware of the writings of Robert Rosenthal and his associates on the effects of expectation. *Pygmalion in the Classroom*[17] has been praised for the hope it offers for what Bernstein referred to as our "little deficit systems," and it has been savagely attacked as scholarly trash, or worse.

I do not propose to argue the case for expectation as a factor in school performance or that expectation is communicated, often without conscious awareness. I assume these to be more or less axiomatic. Supportive research evidence is impressive in areas other than that of the school. To reject expectation as a factor in academic ability and achievement of students is to exempt the formal educational process from law-like effects of anticipation of delayed responses.

What we may not realize is the extent to which we build expectation into the curriculum by our staffing and sorting procedures, by the various indices of student attributes that we employ in our educational system, and by our storage for retrieval of these student indices. By tracking students according to aptitudes or abilities *we administratively establish expectation of student performance.* By our system of cumulative records of

15

student performance, we store expectation-setting information for ready retrieval. By staffing our schools from the middle class at the policy-making, administrative and classroom teaching levels, we set social class standards of student behavioral expectation. Just imagine the expectational consequences when school counselors may have instant display of computerized profiles of various quantitative indices of individual students. The sophistication of such a display can easily distort and displace the living human being facing the counselor.

The point I am making is that our whole educational system operates to transmit messages on the scaled worthiness of the individual student, that these messages are clearly read by both students and parents as well as by teachers, that these messages help to establish teacher expectations on the one hand, and student self-images on the other. The communication system institutionalized in education actually is highly complex, highly efficient, and highly self-defeating. Its redundant messages are designed more to inhibit than to nurture growth, more to maintain than to change the status quo, more to enforce conformity than to release creativity.[18]

The tired cliche of a breakdown in communications is a disservice in general, and particularly so when applied to the field of education. The problem in education is not with the communication system as such, but with the messages it transmits so efficiently.

Remoteness of the Tutor. Major technological developments in education involve, among other things, (a) increasing remoteness of the tutor from the tutored, and (b) increasing control over the structure of educational communication by the remote tutor. The textbook, the filmstrip and motion picture, and, more recently, television, all involve remote message sources. All standardized tests involve remote source and control, and standards of evaluation of student ability and performance.

Remoteness of message and evaluation sources is not new. The first major breakthrough in total control over instruction by a remote source came with the commercialization of programmed instruction. Individually prescribed instruction is an extension of programmed instruction over time, in scope, range of alternatives, and degrees of differentiation of levels and substance of content of the formal curriculum.

The superficial effect of these latter developments is to reduce the autonomy of the teacher in control over instructional messages and in major areas of classroom management, and simultaneously to enlarge the teacher's clerical functions and activities. In a recent study, it was reported that this creates uncertainty among teachers as to their professional role, lack of clarity as to what is expected of them, and feelings of anxiety![19]

They also report two more fruitful reactions: (a) teachers realize that they need more training if they are to cope successfully with individualized instruction; and (b) they encounter in an individualized curriculum a challenge to their creativity as teachers. In other words, individualized instruction is "good for the teacher." It reveals their need for a higher level of professional competence, and it calls into play what Arthur J. Brodbeck of Pennsylvania State University[20] calls "the silent brain," the unused 60 per cent of the mind which lies beneath the thin surface of consciousness and provides the well springs of creativity.

Remoteness of tutorial control from those tutored carries with it at least two risks. One, message content, structure and display are likely to be determined by white, middle-class tutors, thus preserving in the curriculum the unreality of the kindly-postman-and-white-picket-fence culture. Two, local control of education, which has been a somewhat illusory tradition brought suddenly to life by protests against the irrelevance of the school to life style and life goals among the poor and the disrespected, is prohibited by a remotely controlled, highly prestructured curriculum.

Privacy of Teacher-Student Relations. Within the traditional school, communication is face-to-face between teacher and students. It is largely public. What is said on a person-to-person basis is heard by all others present. Classroom communication is also highly teacher-dominated; i.e., the teacher does most of the talking. This last fact is the basis of much of the criticism of instructional television. It is still teacher talking, and it violates the face-to-face expectation in instruction.

Face-to-face student-teacher relationship is one of the impervious mythics of teaching and tutorial learning. Face-to-face student-student relationship is also included in this mythic. This latter relationship is at the heart of the movement for racial integration. Apropos of this, both Coleman[21] and Christopher Jencks[22] propose that among Negroes, but to a lesser extent among whites, students learn more from their peers than from their teachers. I do not want to make this a controversial issue. I merely want to point out that face-to-face communication occurs between role levels and within role levels.

Looking ahead to the directions of diffusion of innovation in education, it seems clear that individualized instruction (in one format or another) is in a growth stage. It is the strategy, rather than the idea, of individualized instruction that is novel. What we are dealing with here, consequently, is concept momentum rather than the inception of a primitive concept in classroom management.

With individualized instruction, interpersonal communication is likely to undergo three major communication pattern changes. One, peer group intercommunication may be reduced or restructured for the simple reason that there is less in common to talk about academically when students are in different stages of the curriculum structure. Two, teacher-student (and where physically provided for, student-student) intercommunication may change in situational setting and substantive character from public to at least the semi-private, and in many cases, private basis. Three, in private communication a change in pattern also comes, I suspect, in non-verbal communication behavior.

Decibel level of speech is likely to decline drastically. Body posture is likely to be more relaxed. Spatial distance between teacher and student is dramatically reduced. Physical contact is more permissive and likely to be more playful and more expressive of personal acceptance and encouragement, or of rejection.

Media Messages. Media do indeed carry their own messages. Rather than condemn Marshall McLuhan for his slogan, "The medium is the message," as so many academics are prone to do, it seems the better part of valor to try to understand what he is saying and to refine and, if necessary, reformulate his propositions.[23]

The importance of reading cannot be over-emphasized. The mind of post-Gutenberg man may have been informed by the medium of print—that his sense of detachment and of sequence, linearity, uniformity, and regularity may not be the product of accelerated evolution but of the technology of communication.[24] It is particularly interesting that the late Gary Steiner, in his

The People Look at Television[25] found a positive correlation between amount of schooling and the sense of worthwhileness of reading—not necessarily reading Great Books, but just reading. A negative correlation was found between amount of schooling and appraisal of television. The implications of this attribute of schooling are so apparent that they require no further comment.

I have the impression that multimedia usage in education is so widely accepted in the abstract that it needs no propagandizing. I have a few reservations, however, on the subject of multimedia usage:

(a) When we say that each medium should be used for what it does best, we are begging the question. We don't really know, except on an armchair basis, either what each medium does best or how to maximize what each does best, if and when we clearly identify the unique functions of each medium.

(b) Some of the multimedia demonstrations I have seen amount to little more than sensate cacophony. If that is what is wanted, the discotheque is the place to find it, and the place where it belongs.

(c) In our concern to structure the curriculum efficiently, let us not forget that some of the media; e.g., the motion picture, does or can produce a continuity of experience and a simultaneity of effect, or what the late Hadley Cantril called a *stimmung*, or mood. There is, of course, a place for the film loop, the concept film, and the tape cassette, but these are not the only ways that film and tape are packaged, or should be.

(d) Regardless of the extent to which it reached and touched our "little deficit systems," the critically acclaimed, public relations-promoted TV program, "Sesame Street" more than any single event, has saved the face of instructional television and of NET.

The Value Spectrum. Again and again we encounter in literature on education the statement that the school is a moral enterprise. By this it is meant that schools are intended to do good, to make things better, to improve the quality of life. This, in part, is the reason for the stigma attached to the dropout as a rejector of the good, and the value attached to the diploma and the degree as a certificate of self-proving in pursuit of the good.

If we accept the moral purpose of the school, as I do, then we must confront some corollaries which it is more comfortable to sweep under the rug. These corollaries may be drastic in their implications but simply cannot be dismissed because they are difficult to deal with in practice.

1) The moral function of the school in a changing society is not to transmit the status-quo value system of a society in deep trouble, but either to change the order of value priority or to organize the value structure on the spectral rather than the hierarchal principle of values.

2) Values are internalized not so much on the basis of what people say but what they do; i.e., the operational norms of behavior of reference groups or models.

3) As the front-line agents of the school, teachers have as their first order of business the serious, searching examination and necessary reordering of the values they act out in their role as teacher.

Within the white middle-class value system, respect is regarded as something to be conferred for personal worthiness. Being middle class means behaving with such personal worthiness as to earn respect in the community. Being a working man, being poor, being black, being Puerto Rican, being Mexican-American carry their own tags of disrepute on the children, and these tags create low levels of teacher expectation of both life goals and academic achievement.

I really do not think that any of our promising technologies of instruction is going to make very much difference in performance levels of our school systems until we learn to respect human beings simply because they are human, until we set higher levels of expectation, free of class, color, and dialect, and until we communicate this human respect and higher expectation to our students. We can do no better than heed words of Edgar Dale:

> Life is not a hundred-yard dash; it's a long-distance race. It's a race against sloth, ignorance, apathy, the willingness to take things as they are and leave them that way. But if we are to take things with gratitude instead of for granted, we must spend some of our time contemplating where we are and where we are going—or drifting.[26]

NOTES

1. Lynn White, Jr., *Machina Ex Deo: Essays in the Dynamism of Western Culture* (Cambridge: The MIT Press, 1968).

2. John Holt, *The Underachieving School* (New York: Pitman Publishing Corp., 1969).

3. Edgar Z. Friedenberg, *The Dignity of Youth & Other Atavisms* (Boston: Beacon Press, 1965).

4. Philip Jackson, *Life in Classrooms* (New York: Holt, Rinehart and Winston, 1968).

5. James S. Coleman *et al.*, *Equality of Educational Opportunity* (Washington, D. C.: U. S. Government Printing Office, 1966).

6. Arthur R. Jensen, "How Much Can We Boost IQ and Scholastic Achievement?" in *Environment, Heredity, and Intelligence*, Reprint Series No. 2 (Cambridge: *Harvard Educational Review*, 1969), pp. 1-123.

7. John Demos, *A Little Commonwealth: Family Life in Plymouth Colony*. (New York: Oxford University Press, 1970).

8. Eleanor Burke Leacock, *Teaching and Learning in City Schools: A Comparative Study* (New York: Basic Books, 1969).

9. Basil B. Bernstein, "Education Cannot Compensate for Society," *New Society*. February, 1970, pp. 344-347.

10. Philip Jackson, *The Way Teaching Is* (Washington, D. C.: National Education Association, 1966).

11. Commission on Instructional Technology, *To Improve Learning* (Washington, D. C.: U. S. Government Printing Office, 1970).

12. Anthony G. Oettinger, *Run, Computer, Run: The Mythology of Educational Innovation* (Cambridge: Harvard University Press, 1969).

13. Charles F. Hoban, "The Dilemma of Adult ITV College Courses," *Educational Broadcasting Review*, June, 1968, pp. 31-36.

14. George Gerbner, "On Content Analysis and Critical Research in Mass Communication," *Audiovisual Communication Review*, Spring, 1958, pp. 85-108.

15. Charles F. Hoban, "Or and Curriculum Planning," *Audiovisual Instruction*, March, 1968, pp. 263-266.

16. Philip Jackson, *Life in Classrooms*.

17. Robert Rosenthal, and Lenore Jacobson, *Pygmalion in the Classroom: Teacher Expectation and Pupils' Intellectual Development* (New York: Holt, Rinehart and Winston, 1968).

18. Eleanor Burke Leacock, *Teaching and Learning in City Schools: A Comparative Study.*

19. John M. Flynn, and Clifton B. Chadwick, "A Study of Teacher Role Behaviors in an Innovative School," *Educational Technology,* February, 1970, pp. 49-55.

20. Arthur J. Brodbeck, "What is a Human Potential Program?" The Pennsylvania State University (Offset), February 11, 1970.

21. James Coleman, *Equality of Educational Opportunity.*

22. Christopher Jencks, "A Reappraisal of the Most Controversial Educational Document of Our Times," *The New York Times Magazine,* August 10, 1969, pp. 12-13, 34-36, 42, 44.

23. Marshall McLuhan, *Understanding Media: The Extensions of Man* (New York: McGraw-Hill Book Co., 1964).

24. *Ibid.*

25. Gary Steiner, *The People Look at Television: A Study of Audience Attitudes* (New York: Alfred A. Knopf, 1963).

26. Edgar Dale, *Can You Give the Public What It Wants?* (New York: Cowles Education Corp., 1967), p. 219.

Commentary

Harry A. Johnson

Dr. Hoban omitted some of the points which I think are quite important. I would like to comment on the statement about the family defense. I think that it is an important one because, unfortunately or fortunately, as we look at ourselves in American society, we Negroes have to deal with ourselves from many vantage points, vantage points that are not quite so clear to others. Dr. Hoban states, "Lower socioeconomic status frequently demands family defense against the onslaught on children and youth at the hands of our class-oriented school systems." Well, we as a family, or our families, have not only a defense against teachers and middle-class values, but we have a defense against what we might call a race-oriented society. I do not think most good-feeling Americans really know how race-conscious Americans are. It permeates every single act.

Now about teacher expectation. We are very glad that this is coming to the front, that people are giving a great deal of attention to it now. And this is coupled with another point in the paper regarding IQ. I think that every parent, and especially black parents, should reserve the right to conceal from *any* teacher his child's IQ. Because it is one of the most dangerous weapons in the hands of an ignorant, poorly informed teacher. As far as expectations are concerned, I think that teachers will have to begin to get some kind of training in how to deal with children outside the context of expectation. That is, I think they need to be well aware, or made aware, of the problems that all, especially minority children, face.

The paper also addresses itself to the point that children will have less opportunity to converse with each other about academics when individualized instruction becomes a fact. Since they will all be at different levels, there will be nothing to talk about. In my opinion, they do not talk much about

Harry A. Johnson is a professor of education at Virginia State College.

academics as it is. If they do, it is in a very superficial way. A boy wants to say to a girl, "You're in my algebra class; what was that problem number three?" He starts walking with her, but who cares about what problem three was or is? I think that what will happen is just the reverse, that each will be at a place that he owns. He will feel excitement because he owns it, and he will feel freer and want to talk about it more because it is his. That is the kind of thing that will happen when individualized instruction becomes a true reality.

The key question for all of us concerned with language is this: Are we enhancing and improving the free flow of ideas in our classroom and outside of it? Are we increasing mutuality, friendly association? Are we giving boys and girls, young men and young women an opportunity to associate with and to develop a zest for excellence?—Edgar Dale, "What Is English For?", *The News Letter*, Vol. XXVI, No. 2, November 1960.

Revolution In Education
Robert J. Havighurst

There is so much loose talk about revolution today that one must define his usage of the term if he wishes to use it at all. In the midst of rapid social change, uncertainty in people's minds as to how to cope with changing problems and opportunities, and an enormous diversity of projects and proposals for improvement, it is difficult to distinguish between revolution and confusion.

I shall define a revolution as a period of rapid fundamental change, with pervasive results. With this definition I do believe that the 1970's will be a period of revolution in education. The forms and practices of education depend on the political, economic, and ideological characteristics of a society. Therefore an educational revolution is likely to occur in response to changes or revolutions in these other aspects of society.

There are three concurrent basic revolutions in American society which are causing the revolution in education—the political revolution, the economic revolution, and the revolution in communication.

Robert J. Havighurst is a professor of education at the University of Chicago.

The Political Revolution

The twentieth century is the scene of the "revolution of rising expectations" of the poor people and the former colonial peoples of the world. It is also the period which future historians will mark as the ending of the Caucasian hegemony which lasted from approximately 1450 to 1950. A colored nation defeated a white nation in war in 1905—Japan defeated Russia. China emerged as a revolutionary world power, after 1950, to challenge Caucasian military and eventually economic power. India became independent. The African colonies became independent.

Within the United States the colored minorities gained a degree of political and economic power, and the civil rights of Negroes, American Indians, and Orientals were officially recognized. At the same time the Puerto Ricans and Mexican-Americans gained economic power, and the poor people generally came into a greater degree of political power.

All these changes have produced changes in American education, and are about to produce greater changes. The goal of racial and economic integration of young people in schools has been officially accepted, though not in fact implemented to any great extent. Still, there are now a million black children attending schools in the South with white children, where there were almost none ten years ago. And since 1960 the proportions of black high school graduates and college entrants have increased more than these proportions for whites have increased. Furthermore, the teaching in our schools about race has vastly improved, as has the teaching about international relations.

The Economic Revolution

During the twentieth century the United States has developed from an economy of scarcity to an economy of abundance. The real income of the average person has increased greatly, while the time he must devote to productive work has been reduced by more than 30 per cent (measured in hours per week) and by almost 50 per cent (measured in lifetime hours of work). During the same period the nature of work has been revolutionized. There are fewer jobs in the labor force which require sheer physical effort, and an expanded number which require literacy and training. Juvenile jobs have decreased in numbers—so much so that the average youth under eighteen has great difficulty finding a job—and we have coined a term to describe the young man who has failed at the major task of adolescence—he is a dropout. At the beginning of the century, almost everybody was a dropout—only six per cent of youth graduated from high school—but a high school education was not considered necessary for adult competence.

Probably the most pervasive effect of the economic revolution lies in the attitudes of people toward work and the use of free time. In the recent centuries, work has been a mixture—in the minds of most people—of toil and ethical behavior. Now it has lost much of those qualities for many people. Work is no longer toilsome for most people, and a growing number of people no longer see work as the best way to serve God and one's fellow man. We are at the beginning of a revolution in social and personal values growing out of the shift away from the centrality of work as a value.

As the educational philosopher Thomas Green has told

us,[1] work is no longer the easiest and most direct way to achieve *potency*, the goal of adolescents and adult men and women. To achieve potency in contemporary America, we must make a constructive use of our leisure time, combining leisure with work in ways for which we have few models in the generations that have preceded the one which is now reaching adulthood.

The effects of the economic revolution on education fall mainly into two areas. First, the high schools and colleges have had to expand in order to meet the needs for vocational preparation of the new labor force, and also in order to provide a relatively wholesome social custody for many adolescents who cannot find employment. Second, the educational system is just beginning to react to the problem of wise and satisfying use of free time. No doubt during the 1970's the school and college curricula will increase their emphases on humanities and the arts. No doubt adult education will increase in importance to Americans, as it takes on the task of helping people find new and better ways of using their free time.

Revolution in Communication

The two revolutions just mentioned have brought in their wake a third revolution which we do not see so clearly and do not comprehend with much certainty. This is the revolution in the ways people learn from other people and interact with other people—the revolution in communication.

The need for communication between different kinds and groups of people is greater now than ever before because the political and the economic revolutions have brought diverse people into closer juxtaposition and placed them in a situation where they *must* interact—they cannot ignore one another, or live in self-imposed isolation. This is true within the United States, and between the various nations of the world.

Edgar Dale recently stated the problem in his *News Letter* by reprinting an article entitled "In the Other Fellow's Shoes" which he had earlier published in May 1955. He asked, "Why is it so hard to communicate with other people, to share ideas, insights, and feelings with them? Why don't excellent, tested ideas move easily into the minds and hearts, the conduct of people? . . . Perhaps the most important ingredient in the education of man or child, teacher or preacher, worker with hand or brain, is the ability to enter sympathetically and imaginatively into the lives of others. Unless we can put ourselves in the place of other persons who differ from us in age, sex, education, wealth, race or nationality, we shall not become fully human."[2]

The communication revolution seems to have three important characteristics. First, the major medium of communication has shifted from the printed word to the spoken word on radio, or when a person is speaking on a television or cinema screen. Second, attempts at communication of major importance are taking place between people of different social classes and of different ethnic or national cultures whose language or word usage differs. Third, any given attempt at communication has unique combinations of passion and of reason among the various participants. One may be nearly all reason and respect for facts; another may be full of deep feeling with little or no factual knowledge; a third may have made a skillful selection of facts to support his deeply felt position.

Communication is extremely important today, but it is also extremely difficult for the reasons indicated. Sir Francis Bacon observed that "reading makes a full man, writing an exact, and speaking a ready man." The present communication situation may enhance speaking at the expense of reading and of writing. A TV conversation show, for example, presented Dick Cavett and Stokeley Carmichael. The latter, in his criticisms of the white European-Americans, said that the real natives of this country were Indians, and the European invaders had wiped out an Indian civilization of 58 million persons. When Cavett questioned this figure, Carmichael assured him that he had read up on the subject (applause from the audience). The facts are reasonably well known to students of American civilization. A number of scholars estimate that in the sixteenth century there were about one million Indians in North America, north of Mexico, and about 20 million Indians in Mexico and South America. Today there are almost twice that number of people of Indian extraction who consider themselves culturally "Indian." It was true, of course, that many Indians were killed in conflicts with white man, probably more than the number of whites who were killed by Indians. It is also true that most of the Indian tribal cultures were shattered by the constant conflict with Europeans. But Carmichael's statement is absurd when it is examined in relation to the facts.

If the medium of attempted communication had been the printed word, it is likely that Carmichael's error would have been challenged during the publication process. No reputable publisher would have printed it, without some footnote about its accuracy. Thus readiness has tended to replace exactness in communication.

The communication revolution consists essentially of a confrontation on terms approaching equality between black and white, between well-to-do and poor, between middle class and working class, between young people and their teachers and parents. These pairs of groups, formerly separated by a power gap, now are attempting to communicate with very nearly equal political and moral power. They must succeed if society is to become stabilized and to progress with the tasks of modern democracy.

Under these circumstances, there emerges a major problem of communication because the different groups have different usages of language and different combinations of reason and passion in their attempts at communication.

Analysis of the Communication Problem

When two parties disagree on a matter which is important to both of them, they may discuss the matter and try to reach an agreement, or they may go to court to seek a solution for their disagreement, or they may fight about it. If they discuss the matter and try to reach an agreement, they must attempt to communicate with each other.

When their communication uses a common rhetoric, they can confront each other in a rational way, with a maximum probability of reaching a rational agreement or compromise. This is generally the case when the opponents are members of the same social class in a democracy. They understand each other. They "speak the same language."

But when members of different social classes or different subcultural groups disagree, they often sound more hostile than they really are, because they are speaking different languages. Lower-class Negro boys, for example, often play the "dozens" in their conversation among themselves. This consists of using obscene or profane language about the other fellow's mother. The object of the game is to make the opponent lose his "cool," and show anger. A middle-class boy might have difficulty interacting with lower-class boys in this situation, especially if he were white.

Middle-class people, regardless of their color, tend to speak with control of their feelings. If they wish to disagree with their opponents, they do it in a mild way. They can express hostility, but according to "ground rules" that impose some restraint on their words and actions.

Another aspect of the communication problem lies in the fact that there are actual differences in vocabulary between social classes and between racial and ethnic subcultures, even though they seem to speak the same language. This produces actual misunderstanding sometimes, and at least reduces the adequacy of communication. It also may make one group seem inferior to another if one of them uses a more nearly "standard" language.

The American Negro subculture, for instance, has certain words and expressions not well known to whites of similar socioeconomic status. A motion picture called "Halls of Anger" illustrates this. As part of a program of racial integration, a big city all-black high school received a small group of white students who were bused to the school. The chief character of the story, a black man who teaches English, is visited by a representative of the central administration who is giving vocabulary tests to the students in all high schools. He reads off a list of words, asking for definitions; and the black students are generally ignorant of them, while the two white students in the class can define them. Finally the black teacher, who is trying to establish human relations in his class, pushes the examiner out of the door and continues the "test" with expressions from the local black culture.

The black students can define these words easily, but the white students do not know them.

In the face of these problems of communication, the following typical situations are likely to lead to a breakdown of rational relations:

- A school board meeting at which a group of black parents demand the removal of a white school principal.
- A school principal facing a group of students who are "sitting-in" in his office until he meets their "non-negotiable demands."
- A college faculty committee faced by a student activist group which demands a separate "ethnic studies" program administered by a faculty member whom they will choose.
- A meeting of a teachers' organization in which a "black caucus" demands that 50 per cent of the officers be black.

In such situations the group which was formerly inferior in power is apt to use a rhetoric which sounds hostile and violent, while the "establishment" group may use language which seems to the other side to be weak and uncertain.

Strategy of Confrontation

A reaction in the field of education to the problem of communication is *confrontation strategy*. This seems to have developed out of "sensitivity" training. People of different social backgrounds, different race or different religion, who want to work together but find it difficult to communicate with each other, are encouraged to drop their inhibitions and express their feelings about one another. It is thought that communication of feelings and emotions, once it takes place with little or no inhibition, will lead to more satisfactory intellectual communication.

This strategy is easier for the previously subordinated groups to adopt. They are likely to feel hostile to the establishment, and they can get satisfaction from venting their hostility. The previously superordinate group is likely to hold back and maintain a reserve, thus defeating the effort at communication.

In confrontation, the person or group with the most intense feelings is likely to dominate the person or group who has a more rational approach. Occasionally, however, a member of the establishment combines rationality with passion and becomes very effective with this technique.

I do not see confrontation strategy as a means of producing useful solutions to our educational problems. One might argue, however, that confrontation strengthens the position of the underdog in negotiations for improved education. Anything which strengthens his position and makes him more nearly equal in power to his adversaries is useful, for it means that his interests will be respected and this may lead to a sounder solution of current conflicts than would come out of an attempt at negotiation on his part from a weaker position.

Responses of Education to These Revolutions

During the past decade we have seen the American educational system reacting to these revolutions like a vast, loose-jointed, and cumbersome organism. From the early 1960's when optimism prevailed, we have stumbled our way into a morass of problems and spent enormous amounts of energy and money. Now the optimists are in the minority.

We know that there must be radical changes in our educational system, but we are not sure what they should be. We have tended to ignore the substantial, positive educational accomplishments of the decade in our frustration with our failures.

Criticisms of the Educational System. There has been a good deal of irresponsible and unfounded criticism of public education. It has become popular with such publications as the *New York Times* to write of "the failure of the public school system" as though this was a generally accepted fact which does not require proof. Publications find it profitable to print books and articles which say that "our children are dying" because of the bigness and impersonality of the school system, and the stupidity or maliciousness or prejudice of the teachers.

Critics in one group are philosophical anarchists, followers of Jean-Jacques Rousseau. They are opposed in principle to human social institutions. They believe that society puts people in chains through its forms of government, business, religion, and education. This group is always present and always voluble in a free society. Sometimes it is ignored by the society; but if the society is having trouble, this group gets a hearing.

This group serves a useful gadfly function. It may stimulate the society to intelligent action. But it generally has little or nothing to say about the constructive changes that might be made to solve society's problems. It calls for "revolution for the hell of it," and suffers from the quaint delusion that something much better will certainly arise from the ashes of the present institutions, if only they are destroyed.

Critics in another group are constructive reformers. They look for the causes of the present problem, and then go to work to cure the problem. They believe that institutions are necessary, but must be changed in relation to the changing social situation.

This group needs public support. Some get it, due to a fortunate combination they have of zeal and clear thinking. But the public has difficulty distinguishing between the clear-headed ones and the muddled ones who go in for simple, global panaceas.

Alternatives to the Public Schools. It is popular, just now, to look for alternatives to the existing public school systems, on the ground that these systems are too rigid and bureaucratic to meet the needs for change and experimentation. New models are sought, and public funds are urged to support experimental schools operated by federal or state agencies, by labor unions, by universities, by the army, or by local groups who wish to experiment—almost any entity except a school board.

These would presumably be experimental ventures devoted to developing and evaluating new approaches which might eventually be adopted by the more conventional school systems. As such, they are being supported by private foundations and also by federal government funds.

A more extensive search for alternatives is advocated by a variety of persons through the use of vouchers from public funds given to parents, thus permitting them to search for the kind of education that would work best for their own children, outside or inside the public school system. A useful description and critical analysis of six of these voucher proposals has been published.[3] Some people see this as a means of developing school systems which is a practicable alternative to the conventional public school system. Others see it as a means of fostering experimentation that may contribute to reforms in the public school system. In my judgment, the voucher scheme may be an exercise in futility, but it may be worth limited experimentation.

Radical Experimentation. The most promising activities, in my judgment, are the following experiments which depart radically from conventional classroom methods: (1) Storefront academies for adolescent dropouts, (2) Tutoring by age-mates or by pupils of the same social background but a few years older, and (3) The use of "re-enforcement" techniques and operant conditioning methods with disadvantaged or slow-learning children.

Forms of Institutional Change. Since school systems are clearly not working effectively with socially disadvantaged pupils, it is natural that changes in the institutional structure should be proposed. The proposals take two broad forms. First, it is proposed that the larger school systems should be "decentralized" into smaller systems which presumably are closer to the local communities that make up large cities, and which may not have such large and rigid bureaucratic structures. The best known example of a change of this sort is the New York City School System. After more than two years of study and argument by local organizations, state government, and the State Board of Regents, the elementary schools (not the high schools) have been placed under approximately 30 relatively autonomous elected school boards. Each school board represents approximately 120,000 registered voters, or a city the size of Akron, Omaha, or Syracuse.

The City of Detroit is under order by the Michigan State Legislature to subdivide its school district into seven to 11 autonomous districts, each about the size of the New York districts.

It is difficult to see how these procedures will bring the school system any closer to the local neighborhood community. The division of a city into administratively autonomous districts of 200,000 to 300,000 runs into the danger of hardening the present forms of racial and economic segregation. The new district boundaries in New York City clearly have this effect. Some districts are 90 per cent or more black, some are 90 per cent or more Puerto-Rican, and some are 90 per cent or more non-ethnic white.

Some administrative decentralization may be desirable in big-city school systems, but this can be obtained by simple school board actions, as has been done in Chicago, without erecting legal boundaries that may Balkanize the school system.

Quite a different form of institutional change is the creation of small local community districts of no more than 3,000 to 5,000 pupils, with a single high school and its feeder elementary schools. In a unit of this size there is some possibility for influence by local parents' organizations, and the individual parent can get closer to the source of decision-making. This form has much in its favor, although the extent of power and responsibility of locally chosen advisory boards must be clearly stated and understood.

The New York City experiment, with three such units, will be useful to other communities. Though many mistakes appear to have been made in the New York City cases, they have shown that there are real possibilities for effective improvement in local schools with local advisory boards or committees that have clearly understood functions.

Forms of Educational Change
in the 1970's

Can we predict the major changes that will remake education in the 1970's? Perhaps we can say with varying degrees of certainty that the following changes will constitute the major features of the educational revolution of this coming decade:

(1) A Pre-School Program for Disadvantaged Children. This has been tried and proved in eight or ten different school systems. Disadvantaged children who have had one or two full years of pre-school work have gained at least ten IQ points, have moved into the first grade ready to learn to read, and have maintained this level of learning ability to the third grade. These experimental programs need another year or two of continued evaluation, but it can now be said responsibly that several alternative pre-school programs are available as models for city school systems to adopt and adapt.

At the same time it must be said that no big-city system has yet put a really effective pre-school program into effect. The country-wide evaluation of Head Start programs made by Westinghouse Learning Corporation and Ohio University in the Spring of 1969 showed that those programs on the average were not effective in helping children carry the gains made in Head Start on into the primary school grades.

Thus the large conventional school systems have this task yet to accomplish. They have federal government money available for substantial support of the program, and they have several successful experimental models to follow.

(2) A Mastery Learning Program in the Elementary Schools. The experiments with programmed learning, together with the Mastery Program which Benjamin Bloom helped work out in schools in Puerto Rico, appear to have developed a procedure capable of widespread expansion. The work assignments for the pupil are divided into relatively small units with frequent tests for mastery. The pupil works for the mastery of his assignment and keeps on working until he has demonstrated mastery. No matter how slow he is, compared with the rest of his class, he achieves mastery before going on to the next assignment. Bloom has found that the slow pupils move along *much more rapidly than he had expected.* Not only do pupils learn more effectively; they also come to enjoy learning. Bloom says:

> The clearest evidence of affective outcomes is the reported interest the student develops for the subject he has mastered. He begins to "like" the subject and to desire more of it. To do well in a subject opens up further avenues for exploration of the subject. Conversely, to do poorly in a subject closes an area for further study. The student desires some control over his environment, and mastery of a subject gives him some feeling of control over a part of his environment. Interest in a subject is both a result of mastery of the subject and a cause of mastery.[4]

The essential thing is for the pupil to gain a sense of competence to do school work if he tries hard, and to see clearly at every step of the learning path that he is making progress toward a goal he wants to achieve.

(3) An Expanded School Program in the Arts and Humanities, Aimed at the Realization of Expressive Values. American society is now engaged in the process of changing its major goal from that of productive work to that of using time in ways that maximize human satisfaction and self-realization. Having achieved the distinction of producing the greatest quantity of material goods per worker of any country in the world, we now turn to the more complex task of consuming these goods wisely and balancing work with leisure.

Every American has more leisure time (time free from work) than his grandfather had. Nobody is forced by iron necessity to work as long as his grandfather did at the beginning of the century. This leisure time may be used for a variety of activities, some of which are more strenuous mentally or physically than most work is. We shall increasingly speak of higher and more liberal forms of work and action rather than of work and non-work.

If the business of life is living, with work just one form of living, then the old *ethics of work* on which our society has rested since the Reformation must be replaced by a *broader ethics of the use of time*. These ethics must have standards of better or worse that apply to use of time. The standards will be more flexible and more varied than the ethical standards that have been developed to apply to work.

The new ethics of the use of time will include not only *moral standards* but also *esthetic standards*. This basic change in American values will cause a change in education from *instrumental* to *expressive* values and forms of activity. Instrumental education means education for a goal which lies outside and beyond the act of education. In this form, education is an instrument for changing the learner's situation. The learner studies arithmetic to be able to exchange money and to buy and sell things and to become a competent scientist or teacher. The learner as a young adult studies in his vocational field to get a promotion, or studies cooking to become a better housewife. Instrumental education is thus a kind of investment of time and energy in the expectation of future gain.

Expressive education means education for a goal which lies within the act of learning, or is so closely related to it that the act of learning appears to be the goal. The learner studies arithmetic for the pleasure of learning about numbers and quantities. The learning of arithmetic is its own reward. The learner studies the latest dances so he may enjoy the dances he and his friends attend. He learns to dance "for fun" and not to become a teacher of dancing, or even to make new friends. Expressive education is a kind of consumption of time and energy for present gain.

The schools will reflect this basic change by increasing emphasis on the arts and humanities. Dramatics will become a much more important part of the high school curriculum. Humanities courses will become more popular in the senior high schools. Adult education will stress more and more the expressive rather than the instrumental activities of adult life.

(4) Alternatives to Academic Education for 15- to 20-Year-Olds. The twentieth-century revolutions have profoundly changed the course of life for youth. Our educational response has been to continue their period of formal education further and further beyond the age of 14, until now we tacitly accept the goal of high school graduation for all and at least two years of college for the majority.

One has only to state the goal in these simple terms to realize that either it is impossible or we must redefine the institutional forms and aims of the high school and college. We have been struggling to do the latter, during the past decade, in the face of a 40 per cent increase in the numbers of an age cohort, commencing with the 15-year-olds of 1962, due to the sharp upswing of the birthrate in 1947 and its continuation at a high level until 1960.

With work experience programs, remedial programs, and multi-track scheduling, we have tried to restructure the high school so that it could serve non-academic youth better. When these have not worked, we have used our ingenuity to create store-front academies and other programs to give dropouts a high school diploma or its equivalent.

At the college level we have stretched the college entrance gate to admit students who cannot possibly pass the conventional college-entrance tests for reading, writing, and arithmetic. Then we have created new college programs with lower standards and with greater "relevance" for the youth who have been admitted and who do not find a tolerable place in one of the conventional academic majors.

We are now at the height of the confusion caused by pressing these socially desirable policies into instructional molds that cannot abide them. To get a reasonably stable solution of the problem, we probably will have to create new institutions either within or outside the educational system.

The coming decade will probably see something like the following. As a general principle, it will be agreed and written into law that the state has responsibility for providing educational services to all youth up to the age of 20, unless they are established in the adult roles of stable employment or marriage and homemaking. The educational services may be academic school or college work, useful employment with educational values on public service projects, or apprenticeship. These will be compulsory for those not already in the adult roles that have been mentioned.

The state educational system will have to be expanded to provide these additional services, or a state youth authority will be maintained to share responsibility with the state department of education.

Added to this may be a year of required national service for all youth under 20, with a choice of military service, environmental improvement service, or some other form of socially desirable service. A major problem to be overcome is the danger of segregation of youth by socioeconomic status and race into different types of programs. This problem can be solved much better than it is being handled today, but it will always be a problem.

(5) A Metropolitan Area Educational Authority. The problem of central city versus suburb which became acute during the 1960's includes the problem of the central city school district and its surrounding suburban school districts. These have fostered racial and socioeconomic segregation, inequality of financial support, and inefficiency in the use of resources for education.

It seems clear that the suburbs and central city will have to cooperate more fully in most of the functions of government, including education. This cooperation may be partly voluntary, but some of it will become formalized through government. The next 20 years will see a steady evolution of metropolitan area government and educational action.

The great need in terms of school system structure is for a single metropolitan area authority which finances the schools of the entire metropolitan area equitably, and brings the various school systems together for area-wide planning and research into area-wide problems, and into cooperation on matters which they can handle better in common than individually.

The social and physical renewal of the cities should proceed with the fullest participation by the school system. The renewal of the cities should be a metropolitan area operation since the central city and the suburbs are in continual interaction, and anything that happens to the central city affects the suburbs and vice versa.

This does not mean that local school boards will be taken over by a single metropolitan school board. Local boards will continue to handle local educational matters. The optimum size of a local school district will be worked out on the basis of experience. The appropriate locations of various kinds of decisions about education will be found, and the term "decentralization" will come to have a useful meaning rather than being a shibboleth. Local neighborhood responsibility for local schools can be worked out through advisory committees with clearly defined functions.

To speak of this kind of evolution of the complex administrative machinery for a rational geographical unit of a modern urban society as part of an "educational revolution" may seem a misuse of language. It will have to come slowly and it cannot be imposed by arbitrary use of authority. But the political and economic revolutions of this century have made it a central necessity, and it deserves the most thorough research by educators and the most critical but devoted support by citizens.

NOTES

1. Thomas Green, *Work, Leisure, and the American Schools* (New York: Random House, 1968).
2. Edgar Dale, "In the Other Fellow's Shoes," *The News Letter*, XXXV, No. 5 (February, 1970).

3. Ray A. Carr and Gerald C. Hayward, "Education by Chit: An Examination of Voucher Proposals," *Education and Urban Society*, II (February, 1970), pp. 171-191.

4. Benjamin S. Bloom, J. T. Hastings, and G. Madaus, *Formative and Summative Evaluation of Student Learning* (New York: McGraw-Hill, 1970), p. 56.

Commentary

William Van Til

In any speculation on the future, two indispensable and potentially contradictory components must be taken into account. One component takes the form of long-range trends and forces. These can perhaps be visualized as curves moving into the future. Such curves are modified and influenced by other trends and forces, but can be extended into the future by projection and extrapolation. It seems to me that Professor Havighurst has done this very well by looking ahead at the curves for the future of, for example, the pre-school, of learning mastery, of increased emphasis upon arts and humanities, of growing opportunities for young people in the metropolitan area.

But I would like to call attention to another component in reasoned speculation concerning the future. This is the element of surprise, of breaks in continuity, of novelty, of twists, of turning points. Kenneth E. Bolding calls this component "the system break," an expression which I will borrow. The system break-through introduces novel elements and often plays havoc with our conventional wisdom based on the arching curve into the future.

As I read scholars of future planning, the second component, emphasizing surprises, discontinuity, and turning points, includes the following possible system breaks: One of them might be global devastation through nuclear war, reducing broad areas of nations to rubble and exterminating large sections of the world's population. Another possible system break could be world-wide famine growing out of a tragic unchecked population explosion to which the blindness of our political and spiritual leadership has unwittingly contributed. A third turning point could be computer-related technology becoming so influential a force that it revolutionizes our technological and social arrangements. A fourth system break

---

William Van Til is the Coffman Distinguished Professor in Education, Indiana State University.

might be a biological transformation of man through transplants, drugs, chemicals, and other agents drastically affecting the longevity, potentiality, and behavior of human beings.

To this list of system breaks, any one of which has the potential to wreck havoc with any of the extrapolated curves in the future to the point that all bets may have to be called off, some would add the possibility that another system break is presently under way in the United States of America, as well as elsewhere in the world. I am not going to attempt to title or label that system break, because I find that I introduce hangups into a discussion by giving it a name. I'll ask you to give it whatever name you yourself want. The poet William Butler Yeats beautifully expressed what I have in mind when he said:

Things fall apart, the center cannot hold,
Mere anarchy is loosed upon the world.
The blood-dimmed tide is loosed, And everywhere
The ceremony of innocence is drowned;
The best lack all conviction, while the worst
Are full of passionate intensity.

Yet it is still necessary, and indeed mandatory, for us to continue to look ahead, attempting to see the things most likely to develop, including the possibility of a system break. We might well do this in the spirit displayed by Dr. Havighurst, essentially pushing forward some extremely important curves into the future. I would like to trace several, with the reservation, of course, that they are all subject to the possibility of the system break: (1) Extensive use of computer technology, flexible scheduling, and programmed instruction as part of a growing electronic network feeding into homes, schools and offices; (2) maintenance of a semblance of local control of education as we move ahead, through local school boards, yet increasing use of curriculum-making processes which will rely on national curriculum projects, on federal governmental curricular influences, and on the demands of nationwide voluntary organizations; (3) increasing urbanization and the large city school, often part of an educational park; (4) use of a coordinating teacher, who will be the key person in a complex including paraprofessionals, clerical assistants, audiovisual technicians, and computer specialists; (5) extensive use of technology for storage and retrieval. At the same time, the future will involve much discussion of value choices, and most particularly how a person should use leisure in a period of multiple competing opportunities. This, of course, is in the direction of Professor Havighurst's art and humanities.

Trends and curves can be projected into the future much as Dr. Havighurst has described them. But no one dare take too lightly the possibility that along with these curves into the future, and sometimes rudely contradicting them, may come the system break in world society.

Stanley M. Elam

Over the years, many of us who are about half a generation behind Dr. Havighurst in age have come to look to him for many things: for realism, for rigorous analysis, for logical consistency, for mature reflection, for calm good sense. He certainly has not been carried away by the fad of the moment. He bases his opinions on what he knows to be true from a life of careful observation and the exercise of keen judgment. These are, it so happens, much the same qualities that we honor in Edgar Dale. Therefore, it goes very much against the grain for me to have to criticize Robert Havighurst's words. My inclination is simply to say "Amen" and let it go at that, because his was a fascinating and useful piece. Since, however, I am cast in the role of devil's advocate, I might as well play it to the hilt.

First, a blanket criticism. I think it is barely possible that Dr. Havighurst's very virtues have led him up a blind alley. More specifically, in his pursuit of a familiar Fury and in his projections of educational change to be expected in the seventies, I think he may have relied too heavily upon the conventional wisdom. What was wisdom a decade ago may not be good enough today. What most of us beyond the age of fifty seem unwilling to accept or admit is the extent of the revolution we are experiencing. I, too, think we have come to the system break which Professor Van Til introduced in his comments.

Dr. Havighurst said that we are in the midst of revolution. He

---

Stanley M. Elam is the editor of *Phi Delta Kappan* and a professor in the School of Education, Indiana University.

defined revolution as rapid fundamental change. He admits that there must be radical changes in our educational system, and then he proceeds as if we could expect nothing more fundamental to happen than an expanded school program in the arts and humanities, implying expressive values. This will very likely occur, but so what?

I think I detect in Dr. Havighurst's five projections for education this fact: he makes them not entirely because he thinks they will be borne out in ten years, but because he hopes that, by conscious recognition of their importance, leaders in education may bring them into being more quickly and more cleanly.

But what are the real problems of our day: What to do with leisure time? What to do with nursery schools and kindergartens? What are ways of teaching kids faster in elementary school? Developing a different work ethic? Frankly, I am a bit disappointed. The problems that face educators in a period of revolution cannot be separated from the problems that face society. Dr. Havighurst recognized this. I'm sorry he didn't follow this perception through to what I think is a logical conclusion.

On the Indiana University campus this past week, it has been popular around the College of Education to say that education students are "too busy to take part in the demonstrations and rallies attending the announcements of the broadened war, or even to participate in the Earth Day activities" of two weeks ago. Secretly, I'm sure, some of the professors must be saying something much more damning, that education students are too docile, too unaware, yes, too stupid to realize what is happening to their country, indeed to their world. One is reminded of stories of what people sometimes do when their house is burning. Out of habit they rush back into the flames to turn off the lights in the bedroom. I do not mean to be a sensationalist; I do not have to. Events are the sensation of the day. I mean only to suggest that we have our priorities all mixed up and we ought to be doing our damnedest to straighten them out.

Do you believe what *Science* magazine has been telling us nearly every week for the past year, that humanity has six to perhaps 16 years to live unless we make an abrupt about-face? Do you think it is unimportant, not education's business, that our political leaders are taking us deeper into an Asian war we cannot win without endangering the whole world? Do you, or

52

do you not agree with Nathan Pusey and the seven other college presidents who tried to communicate with President Nixon to convey the awful sense of outrage and horror the younger generation feels about the trends in national policy? We have an incipient civil war on our hands, and it reflects the deep social revolution to which Dr. Havighurst has alluded. I think the most important work of the school is somehow to find its role in a period of social revolution.

That over with, let us make a less global and more specific approach to the points in Dr. Havighurst's paper. After all, he did not intend to deal with all the ills of mankind, just some of the ills of education. But educators can speak up and be heard! Professor Theodore Brameld and some of the new progressives have just organized a new association with the notion that educators may be in a better position to speak clearly than politicians or industrialists—certainly more clearly than military men, farmers or medical doctors—on what is wrong with our society and how we may escape doomsday.

Dr. Havighurst has ignored what promises to be one of the truly unique education developments of the seventies. It is foreshadowed by what has been happening recently in Texarkana, on the border between Arkansas and Texas. I was there a couple of weeks ago, and I've written about it for the *Phi Delta Kappan*. It is a fascinating experiment in performance contracting and in what they are calling "accountability." This may be a fad, but I think it is a movement that will grow. We already know that by the opening of school next September there will be at least 25 Texarkanas in the United States. Performance contracts have been drawn up for Philadelphia, Portland, Flint (Michigan), and Dallas—even for the whole state of Virginia. What is happening in Texarkana is essentially very simple. It is a method of introducing innovative kinds of individualized instruction to the public school by way of private contractors. The contractor must achieve results or he gets no pay for his work.

I am not wholly in favor of what I saw there. I am not convinced that awarding portable radios and even TV's to get children to learn what they need to know is a viable procedure. I am not sure that giving stock in the corporation that is running the project is the best way to motivate teachers to do what they ought to do. But it is accepted there, and it is being introduced in other places. The age of accountability certainly has come. In it,

I think, we are going to find one of the most interesting developments of the seventies. But no one can say as yet how useful the development may be in the improvement of instruction.

———————————

Education is in a race with catastrophe, but it is also in a race with entertainment. Those who reject the role of teacher say that their job is to inform, not to reform. But all the mass media are *formers.* They use our time, shape our tastes, muddy our ideas or make them clear. We are being changed and are instruments in changing others. It is time that we saw our social responsibilities and acted accordingly. Rome never lacked entertainment, but it was not able to assimilate the cultures which it engulfed or created. We should do better.—Edgar Dale, "Education or Entertainment?", *The News Letter,* Vol. XX, No. 5, February 1955.

It Seems to Come in Waves

Wilbert H. Pearson

In these days there is something faintly absurd in the social convention of "making a speech." Someone stands up and proceeds to try to use the various organs designed eons ago for biting, breathing, resolving images, and shading his eyes, as means for sophisticated communication.

What comes out is words, supported or hindered by tone, expression, and gesture. But the eye and ear of the audience receive and accept information at a rate many times faster than that at which words can be spoken. Long before the speaker reaches his verb, the audience leaps to the conclusion. Then, there are the honest semantic differences, the silent arguments, and preoccupation with the phrasing of perceptive questions to ask as soon as the speech is over. If the speaker should

Wilbert H. Pearson is chief of the International Communications Media Staff, Motion Picture and Television Service of the U. S. Information Agency.

use a vivid word, or one not present in everyone's active vocabulary — for instance, "holograph" — instantly members of the audience go on Joycean conjugational or declensional trips—holograph, hieroglyph, polygraph, halogen, biograph — and have marvellous visual experiences in estate law, Egyptology, medicine, chemistry, and even a short trip to the movies. And, meanwhile, back at the rostrum. . . .

Until there are reliable systems for finding significant images on film and tape and other substances, wherever they may be in the world, removing barriers to their circulation and use, assembling them promptly and economically into meaningful patterns, and having all the facilities readily available for showing the result to the audience . . . only then could there be a simple correct answer to the social invitation to "make a speech." It could be, "Not on your tintype."

So may I suggest for the purposes of discussion lifting the lids on three related boxes, separately labeled: Perception (Primitive), Revelation (Serendipital), Revolution (Titanic).

Perception (Primitive)

Jane Goodall, the British anthropologist, spent several years among wild chimpanzees in Africa. One sequence of the film *Miss Goodall and the Wild Chimpanzees* finds the chimps coming upon a mirror for the first time. Each of them seems to turn abruptly away from the reflected image, except one. She studies her image in the mirror, seems to try to communicate with it, and then carefully looks *behind* the mirror to see where it is coming from.

A film from Innsbruck in the early fifties was a demonstration of perception, from which was generated a whole family of perception films. Dr. Irwin Moon of the Moody Institute of Science developed and dramatized the idea in "Sense Perception." We already knew that light delivers the outside world upside down to the retina, and the "mind" turns it right side up. Dr. Moon had special spectacles ground to invert the image again, and masked his eyes to block peripheral vision. Within a few days, he began to see right side up through upside-down spectacles. In this condition he rode a motorcycle and flew an airplane (with full safety precautions). Then he removed the spectacles, and saw the world upside down for several days before the "mind" inverted the image of "normal" vision.

Dan Weisburd last year made a film for John Sutherland Productions called *A Sense of Hearing.* It went far beyond the exploration of the physical mysteries of the inner ear and demonstrated with startling clarity how a myriad of sounds (from the chirp of a cricket to the thud of a jackhammer) are associated with visual impressions, filed away in the mind, and instantly recalled visually when the sound is heard again.

Recently, I was having lunch with a physicist who was also chancellor of a university. He had just got out of the hospital after having an operation to improve his hearing. It was called an osteotomy, and involved drilling through the bone. He said to me, "I am about to have a very curious experience. When I taste this beefsteak, it may be like pickled beets or beans; the mashed potatoes may taste like celery or lime; the water, may be like beefsteak or mashed potatoes. I never know." He shook his head. "I called the doctor in some panic when I first discovered this, a couple of days ago, and he said, 'Oh, I forgot to tell you, we inadvertently damaged a nerve that sends taste signals to the brain. But don't worry, the nerve fiber will regenerate and you will soon be back to normal!'" Later I checked with the physicist and his taste has indeed returned to normal.

Revelation (Serendipital)

For centuries, learned men and other tourists stumbled around in the ruins of Stonehenge and fabricated a demonology about the ancient Druid temple. Comes a synergetic relationship between an insightful young mathematician, a computer, and a television camera, and we saw and heard proof that the Druid temple was not a temple and was not built by Druids. It was in fact an observatory, constructed perhaps a thousand years before the Babylonians had "invented" a system of astronomy. But there it was, with the sun rising precisely over the heelstone at the summer solstice for all to see, with learned men on camera protesting that it could not be so.

The French novelist, Colette, sitting in a darkened cinema with her husband, was seeing time-lapse photography for the first time. As she saw on the screen the simple miracle of plants growing, the patterns of stems and leaves and blossoms fulfilling the destiny of their lives in a few seconds, she grasped her husband's arm and exclaimed, in great excitement, "There is only one creature! Do you hear, Maurice, there is only one creature!"

Several years ago it was my privilege to show a program of science films to members of the senior faculty of a large university abroad. The president of the university, a famous physicist, upon seeing the animation in *Tiros—Experimental Weather Satellite*, said, "This is marvelous; it gives me a concept of magnetism I never had before!"

An American university chancellor, seeing the State University of Iowa-American Institute of Biological Sciences single-concept loop film *Gamete Transfer in the Bryophites*, made another discovery. "Look," he said, "It's not random, it's not random at all. It's part of a pattern."

Perhaps more often than we realize, an instant of insight provided by a film sequence may have a profound effect on an individual who discovers some truth or principle from an image on film, simply because he had never looked at it that way before. Every time new information of significance comes to the mind, a new holographic pattern is created, the relays start to chatter, the files are shaken up, information has to be resystematized, connotative and denotative systems rearranged, and a new syntax may be developed for use in the creative process.

We assembled Miss Goodall's chimps, the upside-down glasses, the way hearing seems to code, file and recall images, how one physicist discovered in highly personal terms that the world of taste is not in his lunch but in his mind. What happened? Maybe nothing. Perhaps someone wonders, "Isn't it time we paused to validate what comes to our nerve ends, begin to think in terms of what is coming to us in waves, what may be tangential to this plane of existence, what it would mean to take a look behind the mirror."

What about the notes on Stonehenge, Colette's discovery that it's all one creature, the excitement of finding that a biological process was not random, the re-evaluation of a new concept in earth magnetism? Are they related in any way other than that the camera was involved in the discovery?

Some will say only because the camera in each case was an agent in the process of discovery, and the revelation was on film. In the revelations of discrete and different phenomena are camera and film serving only as a window from one discipline to another? Or is there some deeper current flowing, with the camera and the film the indispensable interpreter?

Revolution (Titanic)

Heraclitus, by the Aegean, saw clearly all existence as a constant flow. The idea may be such a part of the universal consciousness that every man has experienced it in one form or another, but not until recently has he found practical use for it. Four hundred years ago, Copernicus, Kepler, and Galileo developed the possibly new idea that the earth was not the center of the solar system and the planets move in elliptical orbits. But not until the last hundred years have men found it serviceable and even essential, to see this constant flow as organized interrelated patterns.

Pierre Teilhard de Chardin approached the concept as a theologian and a philosopher. In *The Phenomenon of Man* he observed: "The passing wave we feel was not formed in ourselves. It comes to us from far away. It reaches us after creating everything on the way." (There is some irony in the fact that Einstein and Teilhard de Chardin died less than a week apart in New York City, the latter virtually unknown at that time.)

In a new booklet from the Kaiser Corporation titled *Ecology: The Man-Made Planet,* these themes are developed:

> Although less than a century old the concept of interacting systems—of organic patterns—of which man is only one, has already caused profound changes:

—in mathematics it has led to probability theory and non-Euclidean geometries and anomalous numbers . . .

—in physics to the concept of interacting fields of force, quantum mechanics, and the theory of relativity . . .

—in biology to the concept of evolutionary development of living species, shaped by their interaction with a constantly changing planetary environment . . .

—in psychology to the concept of the unconscious, the subconscious, and the conscious as interacting systems of energy exchanges . . .

—in geology to the concept of dynamic processes of the inorganic, moving like waves of energy through the fields of time . . .

—in genetics to the concept of an "alphabet," endlessly reshuffled, where the dealer is time and the "wild card" is mutation . . .

—in business and industry to the growing use of operations and systems analysis, aided by data processing, computerization and model simulation; the flow and process of things through time . . .

And to each of the above we could add generations of motion picture films from the world over, whole films, segments, series, serving as vectors and interpreters of these concepts.

Professor Donald D. Rogers in *Main Currents of Modern Thought,* March-April, 1969, is quoted as follows:

> The new pattern requires a conversion, we must be born again . . . and honestly, even naively, confront experience with humility and innocence. In the new pattern, time becomes an essential dimension of reality, a "fourth dimension," perhaps, without which all the others lose their character and being.

This kind of time can be measured not by logic nor by clocks, but by biological time or growth as exhibited within the living experience of conscious creatures caught up in the relentless flow of organic being.

Evidences that some aspects of the flow are subject to organized prophecy have been established. Twenty years ago the Rand Corporation of Santa Monica, California, initiated what has become widely known as the Delphi system. A modification of the procedure was applied by the Institute of the Future, as reported in the *Scientific American* in February, 1970. Simply, the researchers in a wide variety of disciplines are invited to predict breakthroughs they expect in their fields, and the most optimistic and conservative dates such breakthroughs may be expected to take place. Then they together correct and refine the estimates, and thus construct on a time line stretching to the mid-twenty-first century, a series of polygons, the peak of each polygon representing the median date at which they could predict a 50 per cent chance of breakthrough. Somehow it seems to work. Then it is possible to relate the predictions to each other, and enhance the chance for serendipities.

A generalization is a plateau where a tired mind rests. Maybe that is why generalizations so often tend to appear toward the end of papers. Instead of making assertions toward which Dr. Wagner and Mr. Rosenberg may feel constrained to be kindly, or feel obliged to destroy, I would rather suggest a few questions which might be included in their critiques.

1) It appears that a kind of random-access carousel projector is operating inside the head showing motion pictures and slides. A word or a sound will produce a quick flash from the storehouse of coded

images (Sense of Hearing). If new visual concepts are introduced from the outside, the mind is apparently ready to make enormous efforts (Sense Perception) to shake up the files, develop new combinations, adjust to the new information. To what extent is the educational film, as vector of new combinations of visual and sound images, an agent of creativity?

2) It appears that a constant process of discovery is going on, as over and over we hear of profound new insights being carried from one art or discipline to another because an idea or phenomenon has been recorded and seen on film. How can the chances for those serendipties be increased?

3) We are beginning to accept (with Heraclitus, Einstein, Teilhard) that the waves we are riding began somewhere in the past, are gathering momentum and direction, and are now beginning to crest. The motion picture camera rides easily through space and time; images are overlaid, multiplied, dissolved, and reassembled at will. How does this special facility relate to the predicted breakthroughs, and to man's realization of his true environment?

Ideas on film come from everywhere in the world. One part of the effort is to find them and help them to move across national boundaries. Some progress is being made in improving their international circulation.

In 1967 UNESCO convened a meeting of experts in Geneva, with representatives from 66 countries and a number of international organizations taking part. The meeting reviewed the application of the Audiovisual Agreement and the Florence Agreement, dealing principally with books and publications. They found them good. They urged more countries to participate. Some experts from developing countries reaffirmed with some passion that the international movement of audiovisual materials is essential to such development.

The seemingly impressive statistics on the international circulation of educational film represent only a start. By far the more important statistics would represent the ideas on film which never leave home, never reach audiences that need them most. It seems, however, that the persistent visionaries have made a start toward fashioning a tool that works.

We have a shortage of "the abrasive man" in journalism, in teaching, and other fields. He is obviously a controversial figure. He disturbs the peace of the affluent suburb and the apathetic city. He doesn't fit in. He creates ripples when we prefer calm water. Once the well-rounded man was the well-educated man. Now we are likely to think of him as a smooth, unabrasive fellow, a nice guy. He revolves in a nice little circle, in a nice suburb, where nice people live—"our kind of people," you know.—Edgar Dale, "Journalism: A New Dimension," *The News Letter*, Vol. XXX, No. 5, February 1965.

Commentary

Robert W. Wagner

It is no accident that many young people today are vigorously and deeply involved in film and photography as a method of expressing what they think and feel, and often seem unable to express in any other way short of aggressive behavior or social withdrawal. Wilbert Pearson described this function of film as "expression of creativity," and as "revelation."

Films also have a revolutionary function, and are a force for change. Every beginning film student who has seen Eisenstein's *Potemkin* is aware that this film was revolutionary not only in filmic art, but also in the sense that it was a political instrument which helped explain and extend social processes already in force. What we are seeing today are the continuing effects of photographs, films, and television as images of change in a revolutionary era. The times demand that we look very carefully at how cameras—photographic and electronic—are being used to reflect and shape human affairs and at the effects of such imagery in nearly every aspect of our lives, public and private.

Whatever the recording medium, the camera is a way of seeing both what is "out there," and what is "inside" the individual as well. The camera is a typewriter, a means for personal expression. It is also a weapon. A professor of law at the Ohio State University, in studying the process and effect of campus disorders, commented: "It would seem that the camera is the most hated weapon by the police, more hated than a gun or a brick." For many of the same reasons, students also often attack those with cameras—police, newspaper and television photographers, and other students alike.

Where cameras are permitted, and where adequate samplings of events are photographed from multiple points of view, there may be reason to hope that for the first time in history we might

---

Robert W. Wagner is chairman of the Department of Photography and Cinema, The Ohio State University.

get closer to a truthful picture of complex human events. In Washington, D. C., during the Candelight March commemorating the American dead in Vietnam, hundreds of people were taking pictures (both marchers "inside" the event, and observers "outside" the event) with everything from Kodak Instamatics to expensive Arriflex motion picture cameras and Nagra recorders. The possibility of having not one, but many points of view represented is now possible in contrast to what has been in the past, a rather limited number of privileged image makers, and a restricted point of view.

Although not a completely recent phenomena, the camera as an instrument actively engaged in the social scene is responsible for increasing the volume and velocity of the "breaking wave" of dynamic and rapid change that Mr. Pearson spoke of. The image-making process is physically part of the electro-magnetic spectrum as well as a physical and psychological extension of the human perceptual and communication system.

I would, then, only amplify Mr. Pearson's important point that film is a way of developing insight. While many of his references were drawn from the physical sciences, he would unquestionably agree that film has contributed invaluable insights into the human condition as the probing camera explores the racing, kaleidoscopic landscape of today's social realities. Such events are so complex and move so rapidly that we seldom can arrest them long enough and analyze them reliably enough unless our human perceptual system gets the technological assist which makes it possible to store them up, play them back, and sort them out in some audiovisual form.

The real hazard continues to be the fact that we cannot, because of logistic, technical, and economic, and interpretive reasons, capture more than a sample at best. Such sampling will always tend to be inadequate, because we cannot record everything, nor can we ever report everything with complete objectivity. A photograph or a film will always be a symbolic image taken from the rapidly changing, flowing stream of life, and as such will require supporting "ground evidence" including other images.

There will always be the need for critical evaluation of photographic and motion picture material when used evidentially and especially for "revolutionary" purposes. But the "revelationary" function of these media results when they are used by experienced, responsible and creative image-makers as a means of organizing, simplifying, amplifying and dramatizing otherwise apparently random arrangements, events, or happenings of a disordered world and identifying the elements of unity and universality.

We know very little about the design and effects of multiple-media, multiple-image presentations in education, but at least we are beginning to consider comparative imagery, to explore the dimensions of human perception, and to understand the futility of considering the image-viewing experience as something separate and apart from the "real" environment in which the learner and teacher live and work. The more we explore the expanding concepts involved in imagery and their relationships to the social and behavioral sciences, the more we are forced to consider the *total* communications environment in which people work and learn and respond, and the less validity there seems to be in studies and programs which consider only small, unconnected parts of the whole.

Revelation often precedes and generally follows revolution, and nowhere is the latter needed more than in our present educational system. With the means now at hand, and given the wisdom to use it, it may be that the next "shot heard around the world" will be made not by a gun, but by a camera.

Albert J. Rosenberg

The important thing now is, what is going to happen in the future? When I was first involved in audiovisual education during World War II, the popular theory was that motion pictures were great for educational purposes if the subject required movement. If it were a static subject, a filmstrip would do. We could also use a sound filmstrip if we wanted a "poor man's motion picture." We were told that audiovisual materials were devices for large classes.

Albert J. Rosenberg is vice president of the McGraw-Hill Book Company.

What's happening today? There are some excellent motion pictures using *static* subjects. The subjects could have been done as filmstrips, but not with as much vitality, not with as much music, or as much impact. And I have seen some effective filmstrips dealing with motion. So many of these early theories are changing. The motion picture and the filmstrip continue to be used with classes, but they are also becoming important devices for individual instruction either in the school or, hopefully, in the home of the future.

Filmstrips, recordings, film loops, and study prints are beginning to be located in school libraries as well as in the audiovisual center. Today these devices are available not only to the teacher, but also to the student. Individual instruction has become an important concept for the future.

Audiovisual education is dynamic. It is moving ahead, it is developing many new ideas. However, much more is necessary. We have to try new techniques; we have to develop new materials, new ideas, new equipment; and more important, we have to experiment. My plea is for a cooperative effort. It can't be just the producer, or just the educator. They must be both working together. There will be problems; it is not simple.

In the earlier years there were only 16 millimeter motion pictures. Today we have 16 millimeter, or eight millimeter; standard eight, or super eight. It is silent or sound, magnetic or optical. There are tapes or records, study prints or photographs, even sound filmstrips or silent.

History has shown that the "either-or" concept, particularly in relation to the audiovisual field, is not as important as it seems. All of these materials have found a place in the curriculum, as has most of the equipment. The future of these materials, however, is going to be in the hands of teachers and administrators. Producers and distributors will be willing to do their part by moving into new areas of audiovisual instruction, by experimenting with new ideas, and by setting up new methods. But these materials must do more than just teach. A great many of the materials of the past dealt with facts; we have examples today which deal with ideas. There must be more of these in the future.

Really successful educational motion pictures can compete very easily with television in the home as far as quality is concerned. They can also compete in terms of quality with the motion picture in the theater. However, films must go further.

They must motivate the student to do individual thinking. They must give him insight and understanding about things. They cannot, they must not, be a rehash of other material which can be presented more simply with the printed page or by means of a sound recording.

We also know that we are going to need these materials in a form for individual instruction as well as for group use. We are going to need materials representing different levels of learning difficulty for use in the same subject or in the same class. We are going to need a variety of special materials suitable for the inner-city schools, for the poverty program, for bilingual students, and for special and handicapped students.

With all this, the educator, too, must be willing to experiment in using all kinds of materials and equipment. It cannot be a one-way street. In 1969 we looked at 55 new pieces of equipment that had never been mentioned before that year. This is more than one new item each week. Some of them really were good, but not one of them was useful without educational materials to go with it. And that's where the problem crops up again.

So far as we can see, one of the simplest and best things for the future is going to be the eight-millimeter film, because it is going to give us the opportunity to move into individual instruction. It doesn't matter whether it is silent or sound. We hope that it will be a cartridge so that it will be simplified for utilization and handling. I hesitate even to guess about other types of media. But there's one thing we know is coming very quickly—a change in the method of utilization. Helped by government funding, but also for reasons of effectiveness, films and filmstrips, loop films and recordings, are going to be used by students for reference. These materials are going to be available in the library or learning centers of at least the new schools, and perhaps in each of the classrooms. Audiovisual experiences in the future must be available to the student as easily as any reference book is today. They will be packaged to be small and portable. I have seen some of these inexpensive projectors, viewers, and playback equipment which the student can take to his desk or to a study carrel or even to his home for further study. Our kids are visual-minded today; we have to give them the new materials.

Edgar Dale has pointed out many times in the past the great number of hours that the student watches television or listens to radio, compared to the relatively few hours which he spends in reading. We are finding, however, that the more the youngster uses visual materials, the more he's likely to start reading. There have been a number of research studies showing an increased use of library books following either a program on television or a film in the local theater.

One more big item for the future is the increase both in commercially produced audiovisual materials and in those produced by teachers and pupils themselves. Just as they do their mimeographing or Xeroxing today, so will the teachers and students produce local materials in the future. There will be all kinds of experimentation, such as films without narration to introduce literature, poetry, drama, and to stimulate learning of English and history. There are going to be materials, some animated, that will have far-out concepts to be used in group discussions. There are many such projects going on around the country. But it all comes back to the dedicated teacher and imaginative supervisor. They must do the experimenting and exploring.

One who responds imitatively and without discrimination accepts and conforms to things as they are. The creative responder, however, is innovative, inventive. He lives with one foot out of the groove. To respond discriminatingly requires the ability to see subtleties, nuances, to discover the simple in the apparently complex and the complex in the apparently simple.—Edgar Dale, "The Discriminating Response," *The News Letter*, Vol. XXVIII, No. 2, November 1962.

Higher Education in the Age of Communications

Mitoji Nishimoto

In reflecting upon the past 10 years, or past 100 years, I often wonder what the next 10 or 100 years may bring to education. While we may be able to make reasonable assumptions about coming developments for 10 years in the future, no one is brave enough to suggest what the next 100 years may bring.

Television was very much an infant among communication's media just 30 years ago while radio (although well developed as a commercial industry) was still an educational media "infant." But today, in both your country and mine (and others as well), television and radio are accepted as normal components of instruction by a great many teachers. I first started working with the use of radio in school education 37 years ago. During the early years one of my most difficult problems was trying to convince teachers of the value of

Mitoji Nishimoto is president of the Tezukayama Gakuin University, Osaka, Japan.

radio as an educational tool.

It took eight years to get the Japanese Ministry of Education to recognize radio's value. Even after that was accomplished, teachers, who had themselves been educated in the world of printed materials, were only partly convinced and only half-heartedly cooperated in the use of school radio. Japan began to develop television on a large scale about 19 years ago. At the same time school television programs were initiated. Although the job was a little easier, again I, and other pioneers in the field, had to convince the teachers in the classroom of the value of the new media as an educational tool.

Although I must admit that I am not completely satisfied with the present situation, I may also proudly state that Japanese radio and TV school broadcasts have reached a very high level of development. Today NHK, the Japan Broadcasting Corporation, broadcasts approximately 80 radio and 100 television programs weekly for use in kindergartens, elementary, junior and senior high schools. There are programs covering every part of the curriculum, from science and mathematics to music and art. The most popular of these are used by as high as 80 per cent or more of the nation's schools. In addition to NHK, a number of commercial television stations also prepare and broadcast programs for elementary and junior high school use. In addition to school broadcasts, radio and television programs are broadcast by NHK for use by senior high school correspondence students.

NHK established the NHK Gakuin Correspondence High School in 1963. Only about 75 per cent of the junior high school graduates in Japan are able to enter senior high school. Correspondence education at the senior high school level was established in the early 1950's as a means to enable everybody to secure a complete secondary education. It, unfortunately, attracted relatively few students and graduated even fewer during the first one and a half decades. Following the establishment of the NHK Gakuin Correspondence High School, however, high school correspondence education developed rapidly. Using both radio and television programs as part of their studies, students are enrolled from throughout Japan. The first four graduating classes have totaled almost 6,000 young people from all walks of life, young people who would never have had a chance for a high school education if it had not been for the fact that we in Japan united the capabilities of correspondence education with those of radio and television in presenting a home education program which is both appealing and effective.

I should note, however, that as is the case with school broadcasts, so NHK is not the only source of programs for correspondence students. Channel 12 in Tokyo broadcasts television programs for science high school correspondence use and one university is using FM radio to present programs.

Adult education is another important field where radio and television in Japan play an important part—and it is this field where I have hopes for the greatest development in the future. Radio and television programs for adult and social education have been broadcast since the start of the respective media. Today both radio and television programs are presented for use by youth groups, women's groups, farmers, white-collar workers and many other specific groups. Programs for more general audiences are also part of the daily broadcast schedule.

And yet, unfortunately, except for a very few courses

which are presented for university-level correspondence education, none of these courses lead to any kind of degree, diploma, certificate, or other official recognition of successful completion. The remedy for this is now in the planning stage. The Japanese Ministry of Education, in cooperation with the Ministry of Telecommunication, NHK and scholars, is now preparing to establish a University of the Air. The purpose is to realize equal opportunity for all for a university-level education. We feel that the use of radio and television, in conjunction with correspondence education, is the most practical and the shortest way of achieving this goal.

College or university education may be grouped into three types. The first is the academic course, which the traditional universities have developed over the past several centuries. It might be called the "ivory tower" type of higher education. The second is the technical, scientific and specialist type. Before the Second World War, such education in Japan was carried out by specialized higher schools which rated below universities both in prestige and in academic standing. Following the educational reforms brought about after the end of the war, and also due to the recent rapid advances made in science and technology, these schools are now rated at the same level as the ivory-tower type of universities.

The third type of college education is the study of subjects closely related to practical aspects of daily life and work. Veterinary science, for example, has always been an important subject in the agricultural department of the traditional universities. But it is also an important field of knowledge for cattle ranchers or chicken farmers who have not means or time to attend the university. These people must know the latest and best techniques available for their field, much more than the formal students of agriculture.

They must even go beyond and be able to do research—in other words, conduct experiments in the practical application of the knowledge for the fight against the disease, its prevention, and even for the best methods of cattle or chicken raising. Therefore instruction in veterinary science, placing much more stress upon the practical or application side (in other words, courses like "cattle raising" or "chicken farming"), must be presented for farmers and others through the University of the Air.

This third type of university or college-level education should receive special emphasis by the University of the Air. But the first and second types of instruction are also not to be neglected in its curriculum, because there are many who, after passing the normal age for attending a regular institution of higher learning, look forward still to improving themselves through education. In addition, those who have graduated from the traditional universities and colleges need re-training and new information throughout their lives, not only in the specific field of their activity, but also in a broader cultural sense as well.

Education is really a constant reconstruction of life throughout its entire span and, by means of the University of the Air, students all over Japan will be able to study at a university level, without classroom walls and artificial barriers created by the traditional schools. This is the real function of the University of the Air. It is not planned as a substitute for the traditional universities; it is rather a completely new system of higher education. It is designed to meet the needs of the entire populace—not only those of university age, but also all adults who are striving for a lifetime education.

Use of Radio and Television in the University of the Air

For the first year, an entirely new set of channels for television, completely separate from those already in use, will be alloted and stations will be established in nine major cities throughout Japan. This will permit 50 per cent coverage of the nation. By the end of the third year, stations will be established in each of the 46 prefectural capitals, and by the end of the fifth year, about 260 television stations (including relay stations) will permit 80 per cent coverage. Radio stations, also using new wave lengths, will be built over the same period, and by the fourth year a total of 49 radio stations will cover 70 per cent of the country.

The school year will start in April. This is the beginning of the fiscal year in Japan as well as the traditional academic year. The year will be divided into quarters of three months each: April-June; July-September; October-December; and January-March. Each week during the quarter, a 30-minute radio or television program will be broadcast for every subject offered. The broadcast day will last from 5:00 a.m. to 1:00 a.m. It will be divided into six periods of three hours each.

Theoretically, an almost unimaginable number of subjects could be broadcast every school year—many more subjects than the traditional university can ever dream of offering. Six 30-minute programs can be given during each three-hour broadcast period. There are six such broadcast periods in each day, and the University of the Air will broadcast seven days a week without interruption. Six subjects (per period) multiplied by six periods, make 36 subjects a day; 36 subjects multiplied by seven days a week make 252 subjects; we can offer 252 different subjects during each 13-week quarter. If we mutiply this figure 252 by four, the total number of subjects per year amounts to 1,008. And, assuming that different subjects were to be given over radio and television, it would be possible to present 2,016 entirely different subjects each year. Of course, a great many subjects will be repeated, sometimes during the same day and sometimes from quarter to quarter. So, in fact, the University of the Air will probably never be able to offer as many as 2,016 different subjects a year. But, on the other hand, where is there a traditional university which could begin to match its possibilities?

In addition to the 1,008 subjects possible each year through television and the additional 1,008 which are possible through radio, VTR cassettes can be used extensively. VTR cassettes will allow intra-university use of University of the Air lessons. In addition, individual students can borrow VTR cassette lessons, or the lessons can be placed in special centers, to be made available to anyone. A lesson library of VTR cassettes should be established. Such a library should not be limited to one region, or even to a single country. It should be international in scope. Traditional university and college education in Japan is computed in terms of "units" or "credits" which are granted for each subject completed. A total of 128 units, or 32 units per year, are required to qualify for the Bachelor of Arts Degree. The University of the Air will adopt this same "unit" system. One subject taken for 13 weeks will be worth two units. Some topics, of course, cannot be satisfactorily covered within such a short length of time. These will be spread over a two-, three-, or even four-quarter series.

Assuming that a student decides to take four subjects each quarter, he can earn eight units per quarter or 32 units per year (the same rate as is expected of regular university students) and will be able to graduate within a period of four years. To do so requires that the student listen or watch just four 30-minute radio or television programs each week—something almost everybody could do quite easily. This last statement may have made things sound too easy. Actually each broadcast program will have accompanying correspondence education materials (references and textbooks) for the student to work with, and an end-of-term examination will have to be successfully met before the units will be granted. But this kind of activity can comfortably be done by the student on his own time and at his own convenience.

Another requirement will be the writing of a thesis during the last year of his study. In addition to listening to or watching the programs and studying and doing exercises through correspondence methods, in order to receive a degree each student will have to attend four "schooling" sessions, one for each year. These schooling sessions will consist of two-week courses of study, during which the students will attend regular classes given at one or more central locations. They will be very similar to the tutorials which are planned as part of England's Open University. The schooling sessions will be available eight times a year, primarily during the June-September quarter. Students attending these sessions will have two classes every morning for twelve days (Monday through Saturday, for two weeks) and will thereby earn four units. In the afternoons the students will be able to attend counseling sessions, to participate in group activities, to do work in the library, and so forth.

In planning for the University of the Air, we are relying greatly upon the computer. It will be used, of course, as an administrative aid in handling enrollment records, grading of tests, etc. We are also planning to use it as an aid in analyzing the contents of lectures, and in preparation of manuals and questionnaires. The world has now truly entered the age of computers. The University of the Air should use computers to the fullest extent, in an attempt to perfect instruction—instruction which until now has, by necessity, been handled entirely by the brain of the human teaching staff. I am convinced that the computer will never be able to replace the human and personal aspects of the classroom teacher, but I am equally convinced that the mechanization of the mechanical parts of the teaching-learning process will amplify and strengthen the process as a whole. The use of computers in education is still relatively undeveloped. Their full and active use in all possible aspects is one of the strong points of the University of the Air.

We anticipate the possibility of inviting famous and well known personalities to present radio and television programs to our students. An international faculty can be formed by inviting outstanding scholars from abroad to come to Japan and prepare a series of 13 programs on VTR during a two or three weeks' stay, to be used later by the university. Or, the staff could visit and record the scholars in their respective countries. Although the participation of such well-known personalities or foreign scholars may greatly increase the production cost, a completed program series will be available for re-use in following years. Even if used only once, they will potentially reach more students than is possible today within the material limitations of the traditional university.

The preamble to the UNESCO Charter states that "War is created in the minds of man." We have to mould, therefore, the minds of adults for peace, as well as to develop the mind of younger generations. The University of the Air will be very much concerned with the minds of adults—those minds which control the world's political and economic power. The minds of both the young and the old are important. "Adult power" exists alongside "youth power." The University of the Air, by educating their minds, can change adults and bridge the generation gap which is affecting present-day society, thereby improving the prospects for world peace.

I need not remind you that there is no better way to promote international understanding than to exchange scholars and students among nations. This will be a second strong point of the University of the Air. The university will be open to anyone, regardless of age, who has a high school diploma or its equivalent. Entrance, based upon document examination only, will be as open and available to everybody as possible. My plan is to admit from 20,000 to 30,000 students for the first year. Although the University of the Air is envisioned as a four-year course of study, there will be no time limit placed upon students. They will be able to spend as much time as necessary on their studies, although quick completion will be encouraged. It is anticipated that the Bachelor of Arts degree will be given in one of three levels: Ordinary, Honors, and High Honors. The appropriate level will be determined, based upon the quality of the student's work, his thesis and other performance factors.

The system I have described above is a very new one, and those who have been educated in the traditional manner can hardly understand the rationale behind much of it. This is because they are confined within their own (already learned and set) traditions and concepts of teaching. As they were educated primarily by printed materials alone, they cannot fully comprehend the potentialities of radio and television in education. It is now necessary to convince the more powerful, and possibly even more traditionally minded, university scholars of the value of radio and television in education. Not only that, it is now necessary to show them that education as such need not be carried out in an ivy-covered, ivory-towered citadel.

It is hoped that programs and courses prepared by the University of the Air will be used by the Educational Television Programme International Library and by other countries (both developed and developing) as well as by educational institutions in Japan. Yet there are two large problems that block the smooth realization of these hopes. One is royalties. Royalties have been a large factor in the delayed development of the NHK Educational Television Programme International Library. It is imperative that every nation and every producer of educational programs and materials be as liberal as possible regarding the protection of copyrights and payment of royalties.

The other problem is attitude. The developed countries, for example, need good, current and skillfully filmed and "VTRed" educational materials on foreign lands. The developing nations need the same, plus filmed and "VTRed" basic educational materials for the rapid diffusion of compulsory education among their people. In both cases, however, the attitudes of traditionalists have almost always blocked progress in the desired directions. The technology is available, but the will, the attitude, seemingly is often lacking.

While the ivory-tower concept of university training should and shall continue to exist, the general concept of higher education must be drastically changed in order to meet the needs of the times. Just as the status of technical education in Japan was brought up to that of the ivory-towered institutions following World War II, so the practical education closely related to daily life will also come to be valued highly.

At present, such practical education is little considered by the traditional universities. It is necessary, however, that it be fully recognized, if the University of the Air and the traditional schools are to work together for the good of education. Recent advances in science and technology, and recent changes in the philosophy of modern life, demand that all three aspects—scholarly learning, scientific and technological studies, and learning for practical living—be treated as equals. This applies not just to my country, but to all nations throughout the world. Topics worthy of serious research and capable of a high level of scholarship can be easily found in all those three areas. The last, however, that of practical living, is the least explored and therefore the most fruitful. I dare say that without serious thought being given to the third area, the other two may not advance as rapidly as they should.

Printed materials often put too much emphasis on local or national events. This, in turn, can lead to a narrow-minded nationalism. In contrast, radio and television—because they can be much more current than books, because also they are as mobile as carrying a camera or a tape-recorder—can emphasize events in other nations across wide oceans and continents. Television, in particular, can help in promoting international understanding, because images are always more easily understood among different cultural and linguistic groups than are words that often must be translated if they are to be usable at all.

Books and other printed materials are easily stopped at national borders, while radio and television waves know no artificial boundaries. Canadians living along the border with the United States can easily watch American television, just as Koreans in the southern part of the peninsula can receive Japanese television programs. Radio waves can be sent around the world and radio is playing a large part in making people on both sides of many existing "curtains" understand and know more of each other.

Radio and television can be powerful instruments in bringing peace to the world, through their contributions to bettering education in all the nations of the world, and through their ability to help each nation to understand others better.

Reading is a process of getting meaning from the printed page by putting meaning into the printed page. Reading taste and ability are always tethered to past experience. But reading itself is one way of increasing this capital fund of past experience. Reading, therefore, must be seen as more than *saying* the word, more than *seeing* the sentences and paragraphs. Good reading is the way a person brings his whole life to bear on the new ideas which he finds on the printed page. It is reading the lines, reading between the lines, and reading beyond the lines. It is an active, not a passive, process. The good reader becomes involved with the writing and the writer. He agrees, he argues back. He asks: Is it true? Is it pertinent? What, if anything, should I or could I do about it?—Edgar Dale, "The Reading of Magazines," *The News Letter*, Vol. XXXI, No. 2, November 1965.

Things to Come:
The New Literacy

Edgar Dale

Today there is a feeling of dissatisfaction, sometimes of hopelessness, in the air. We are told that the schools and colleges are not good enough. It is true. We know that the poor are inadequately housed and a plan has been set up (without funds) to build 2.6 million houses a year. Medical care, especially for the aged, is not good enough and is too costly. A Negro woman, Rosa Parks, refuses to move to the rear of the bus in Montgomery, Alabama, and starts a long and continuing series of events all aimed to get long-overdue justice for blacks.

Some of us in the establishment have asked critics of our society to wait, to be patient. "Rome wasn't built in a day," we say. But timetables set exclusively by those in power are not acceptable. Today the speed and nature of change have become a negotiable matter. If the debate is chiefly about the speed of change, why can't we do something to speed up that change? Many of you here believe we can, and see yourselves as architects of a new literacy.

The title of my talk suggests that I will take the role of a soothsayer or an oracle. Soothsayers tend to be dogmatic. Shakespeare has Gratiano say in *The Merchant of Venice* (Act 1, Scene 1): "I am Sir Oracle, and when I open my lips let no dog bark." And I also realize that *sooth* (meaning truth) and *soothe* are closely related, so a soothsayer may tell the truth or gloss over the truth. I'll try to tell the truth and make no Delphic predictions.

For a reason that I do not wholly understand, I love to make predictions of things to come. Perhaps I learned it from my father, who was influenced by the predictions in Bellamy's *Looking Backward* and liked to make them himself. One day when our chain-driven Rambler got stuck in a North Dakota pothole we were pulled out by Clarence Hale, driving a high, buggy-wheeled Ford. As Mr. Hale drove around us, my father said oracularly: "Ed, there goes the car of the future." Years afterward I kidded him about it and asked why he made such a bad prediction. He said: "I never realized that good roads would be developed so quickly." Invention thwarts prediction.

Recently I examined some predictions I made in 1941 regarding the future of the press. I said that ". . . the newspaper . . . of the future will be much more concerned with the desires and needs of its customers—the readers of the newspaper." It *is* happening, thirty years later, but the newspapers did not lead the way. It was led by *Consumer's Union*, by the Consumer Division of the U. S. Department of Agriculture, by Better Business Bureaus, by Ralph Nader, and others.

I forecast in 1941: "The newspaper of the future will be manned by a better personnel." Schools of journalism *have* improved sharply. I predicted that the newspaper would be easier to read, and quoted the *Milwaukee Journal* as saying, "Write the English language. Keep away from *sine qua non, de rigeur, coup d'etat, coup de grace, au fait,* and similar affectations." The newspapers *have* tried to improve readability with the help of Rudolf Flesch, Robert Gunning, and others.

I said that there would be more interpretative writing, noting that: "Interpretation does have disadvantages. When you interpret, you do some editorializing, give your own opinions. Yet the bare bones of facts are likely to be less valuable to a reader than the interpretation of a writer or a press service he has found reliable and enlightening."

I also said: "Labor unions, cooperatives, and religious groups will become much more active in the publishing of daily newspapers." I was wrong. However, the *Wall Street Journal,* with the second largest circulation among daily newspapers in the United States, does an excellent job of presenting the national business and economic situation, offers concrete, easily read stories. The newspapers *make* news by presenting interesting in-depth stories about people who are not *in* the news.

I predicted that: "Radio, television, and other related inventions will continue to have a marked effect on the future of the newspaper . . ." and "Television, too, appears as a possible competitor of the newspaper. Here you won't even have the intermediate step of words. Instead you will see the event itself as it happens or as it was photographed for televising later."

As I looked at my other predictions on mass media, on education, and in the audiovisual field, my chief error was in assuming that the changes would come much faster than they did. My time schedule was off. I predicted in 1946 that we would have cafeterias of learning materials which provided much wider choices for learners. Easy access of this type is only beginning—and this is a quarter of a century later.

H. G. Wells was a predictor of the future and his books provided insight into the future. Think of *The Time Machine, The War of the Worlds,* and his utopian *The Shape of Things to Come.* But in his last book, *Mind at the End of Its Tether,* his ebullient optimism was gone and he saw disaster ahead. Here are his words:

> The writer sees the world as a jaded world devoid of recuperative power. In the past he has liked to think that Man could pull out of his entanglements and start a new creative phase of human living. In the face of our universal inadequacy, that optimism has given place to a stoical cynicism. . . . Ordinary man is at the end of his tether. Only a small highly adaptable minority of the species can possibly survive. The rest will not trouble about it, finding such opiates and consolations as they have a mind for.

Another distinguished Englishman, Sir Winston Churchill, commented on this problem when he received the Nobel Prize for Literature in 1953:

> Since Alfred Nobel died in 1896 we have entered an age of storm and tragedy. The power of man has grown in every sphere except over himself. Never in the field of action have events seemed so harshly to dwarf personalities. Rarely in history have brutal facts so dominated thought or has such widespread, individual virtue found so dim a collective focus. The fearful question confronts us: Have our problems got beyond our control? Undoubtedly we are passing through a phase where this may be so. Well may we humble ourselves, and seek for guidance and mercy.

Our technological society changes faster than people change. Wes Gallagher, general manager of the Associated Press, said on February 20, 1970, that ". . . individually and as a nation, we are not as willing and as quick to change as we once were, but instant news communication and the explosion of knowledge have made quick adoption to new ideas essential."

The times, therefore, call for fast-moving, hard-hitting, flexible programs in business, education, and other fields. Can we develop in time the higher literacy which this requires? For time is running out. Can we use our greatly augmented powers of communication to close this gap? Can we use instructional technology to harness the revolutionary power of a changed industrial and mechanical technology?

The increased power to communicate involves the revolutionary extensions of man himself. Perhaps you associate this term with Marshall McLuhan, but Emerson said in his essay "Works and Days": "All the tools and engines on earth are only extensions of its [mankind's] limbs and senses." He referred to the ocean telegraph, that extension of eye and ear whose performance astonished mankind. He spoke of the possible uses of steam as we would now speak of electrical or atomic power. He thought that Charles Babbage's mechanical digital computer "might calculate interest and logarithms, draw bills and answers in chancery [a high court]."

Samuel Butler's *Erewhon,* written in 1872, says "machines were to be regarded as a part of man's own physical nature, being really nothing but extra-corporeal limbs . . . every past invention being an addition to the resources of the human body." In *The Story of Invention* (1928), Hendrik Van Loon illustrates the tools that are the extensions of man—of his hand, foot, mouth, skin, eyes, ears. The history of man is thus, in this sense, a continuing account of the extension of his senses. Today a man may speak by radio from anywhere and be heard everywhere. Our mouths and ears are also extended by public address systems, recordings, and the microphone.

Our eyes are extended by television, motion pictures, telescopes, spectroscopes, and microscopes. Astronauts bring us superb photographs from the moon.

But these extensions of man must be seen from the viewpoint of the higher literacy. Henry David Thoreau was worried about our insensitive senses, noting in *A Week on the Concord and Merrimack Rivers* (published in 1861) that: "We are comparatively deaf and dumb and blind, and without smell or taste or feeling. . . . The ears were made not for such trivial uses as men are wont to suppose, but to hear celestial sounds. The eyes were not made for such groveling uses as they are now put to and worn out by, but to behold beauty now invisible." To hear celestial sounds and to behold beauty now invisible is an essential part of the higher literacy.

The extension of the powers of man has opened up a Pandora's box of possible choices. Huxley is reported by Walter Lippmann in *A Preface to Morals* as saying: "A man's worst difficulties begin when he is able to do as he likes."

In this society of discordant voices and indecisive choices we are on our own. Growing up in a slowly changing society where grown-ups knew what to do was always painful; the rites of passage were never painless. It was never easy to be an adult when you preferred to be a child or to be an adult when others wanted you to be a child. But today, when parents themselves are bewildered and do not know what to do, the problem is multiplied. Today, even as Matthew Arnold wrote over 100 years ago, we are: "Wandering between two worlds, one dead,/The other powerless to be born."

In a world of poverty and adversity the choices are few. In a world of prosperity the choices are many. In a world of affluence people get a chance to choose to buy what they always thought they wanted, what seemingly had been denied to them. We like to think of adversity as being a source of unhappiness, but prosperity also brings problems for which people are ill-prepared.

Newspaperman Emile Gauvreau, writing many years ago, said in his book, *My Last Million Readers:* "I was now definitely a part of that strange race of people, aptly described in an editorial in the *Herald Tribune,* as spending their lives doing work they detest to make money they don't want to buy things they don't need in order to impress people they dislike."

Ruskin tells this story in his essay "Ad Valorem": "Lately in a wreck of a California ship, one of the passengers fastened a belt about him with two hundred pounds of gold in it, with which he was found afterwards at the bottom. Now, as he was sinking—had he the gold? or had the gold him?"

In today's society we are chiefly consumers, not producers. Once we produced what we consumed, consumed what we produced. What we produced was a part of us, not apart from us. The quality of our output depended on us. Excellence or lack of it was visible.

The Shakers of New England produced much of what they consumed. Their artful simplicity is seen clearly in their furniture. I once asked Brother William, who was making some chairs for us, how he got the wonderful finish. He told that he had selected the wood himself, turned the pieces in his own shop, applied a lacquer, and then he said: "Finally, I gave it the loving touch." What creative counterpart do we have today for "the loving touch"? The Shakers, by the way, were great inventors; but, they had time to enjoy uncluttered space and to gaze enraptured at the lovely Berkshire Hills.

What is it that we lack today to make the necessary "revolutionary" changes to provide access to excellence for all? Is it chiefly the knowledge, the know how? Or a lack of nerve, of will?

We must remind ourselves that possession of accurate information or knowledge is not sufficient to insure change. Knowledge is helpful, valuable, but it isn't enough. The will to change must accompany it. The higher literacy demands that we both know and *do*.

Definitions

I shall use two terms which need definition. The first is communication, the second is literacy. To communicate is to share ideas and feelings in a mood of mutuality. When we share, the communication circle is complete, it is a relationship between and among equals. To the degree that communicators see each other or themselves as superiors and inferiors, real communication will be diminished and sometimes polarized.

In the United States we have long operated by the *consent* of the governed. There is, however, a higher form of communication, namely *consensus* of the governed. To consent is usually to agree to someone else's proposal. What we desperately need are joint agreements, genuine consensus.

I used the term "ideas and feelings." Typically we ignore the emotional element as an important aspect of communication. The school curriculum, furthermore, is in the hands of the verbalists who accent the intellectual process and underemphasize the emotional. Clearly there is a lower and higher element of emotional maturity, of maturity in one's feelings. It involves, for example, the delicacy of feeling necessary to take things with gratitude and not for granted (a phrase of Gilbert Chesterton). It is the ability to appreciate, to be sensitive to subtle nuances of feelings. It is meaningful response to the arts, whether of literature, music, song, dance, home decoration, or whatever the field. John Dewey has defined art as the intensification of the ordinary. It requires the higher literacy to be sensitive to this intensification.

Is it likely that we shall get this higher literacy from the so-called intellectual? Certainly some of it will come from that source. Outside his specialty, however, the intellectual may be an ordinary man, who mistakenly believes that his specialized powers enable him to speak authoritatively on general problems outside his field. Albert Einstein wrote to Sigmund Freud on July 30, 1932, asking a question which deeply concerns us today: "Is it possible to control man's mental evolution so as to make him proof against the psychosis of hate and destructiveness? Here I am thinking by no means only of the so-called uncultured masses. Experience proves that it is rather the so-called intelligentsia that is most apt to yield to these disastrous collective suggestions, since the intellectual has no direct contact with life in the raw, but encounters it in its easiest, synthetic form on the printed page." I conclude that Albert Einstein believed that the intelligentsia were sometimes found among the unintelligentsia.

What do I mean by the term "literacy" and the "new" literacy? I mean by literacy the ability to communicate through the three modes: reading and writing, speaking and listening, visualizing and observing—print, audio, and visual literacy. This literacy, broadly speaking, can be at two levels. First, at the level of training, imitative reaction. Here we communicate the simple, literal meaning of what is written, said, or visualized. I call this reading the lines, hearing the words, or seeing the pictured symbols, and getting the simple, planned meaning from it. We can call this *training,* and I do not use the word wholly adversely. If you were to put the two concepts—training and education—on a scale, a continuum, you would have training at the lower end of the scale and education at the upper end.

Or second, we can have creative interaction, can read between the lines, draw inferences, understand the implications of what is written, said, or spoken. We thus learn what the speaker, writer, or visualizer *meant to say,* which requires a greater degree of literacy. And finally, we learn to read beyond the lines, to evaluate and apply the material to new situations. We use the message in our own varied ways.

I would also classify responses as uncritical and accepting, or as critical and evaluating. The new literacy involves critical reading, critical listening, and critical observing. It is disciplined thinking about what is read, heard, and visualized.

I do not want to overemphasize the propaganda analysis aspect of the new literacy, but it is important. The receiver of communication must reflect on the various messages he is receiving—evaluate their truthfulness, balance, and applicability. I want him to see his daily experiences as possible material for his lifelong filing system, put it into perspective, and use it. I want a much greater opportunity for discussion circles, for feedback or talkback as it has been described.

We face a choice, then, in communication: imitative reaction or creative interaction. If we accept the approach to instruction just described, then we must rethink the terms *teaching* and *learning.* Our stereotype, our present pattern is to have a teacher who teaches and a learner who learns. But even the simplest reflection will show that there is much learning without teaching and much teaching without learning.

Most of our important learning did not take place in school. The child coming to school with a vocabulary of 3,000 words was taught by parents, church school teachers, friends, brothers and sisters, peers and the mass media. Most of all, we are taught by events themselves, if we are literate enough to recognize their meaning. We learn when we ask questions and, when appropriate, we learn by questioning answers. The word *curiosity* is derived from the Latin words meaning *inquisitive* and *caring,* hence, inquisitive caring.

In our schools and colleges the instructors have usually asked the questions. We need to reverse this procedure and have the students ask the questions. Modern technology will eventually enable us to use mediated specialists to answer many of our questions, and then the learner can follow up with questions about the answers. We can now pick up the telephone and ask for the weather forecast, the time, and similar information. But Edwin H. Land, the inventor of the Polaroid Land Camera, has been exploring methods of having students ask questions of a physicist, an astronomer, and others, and to continue the conversation, using a Telewriter as a visualizing tool. Land and his colleagues are developing a way to ask questions of a mediated instructor and to get thoughtful answers.

Obviously we already have this author-reader interaction when we do reference reading. You can ask the compiler of a dictionary what a word means; you can ask the author of an article in the encyclopedia about insects, arachnids, or Arabia. And you will get good answers if the materials have been prepared to answer the predictable questions of children, young people, or adults of varying backgrounds.

Did you ever ask a question of a map and get a poor answer or no answer at all? All of us have. But today's able map-makers and graph-makers are testing maps to discover their communicative power, using student feedback to improve the clarity of the communication. If our instructional materials were better geared to providing clear, interesting answers to the learners' questions, our teachers would not need to spend time explaining poor explanations. All of us need guidance to improve creative interaction in a dialogue. Some discussions, labeled dialogue, are merely verbal ping-pong without a net or a table, so you never know whether you scored or not.

Good dialogue requires good questions. Even able graduate students fumble at first on the analysis of problems which require them to formulate and answer critical questions on specific materials. Philosopher Theodore M. Greene of Yale University once pointed out that the literate man of the future will "master the art of responsible conversation."

New Basis for Education

If we shift the basis of education from having students answer teachers' questions—often ones that the student never asked—and get them to ask their own questions, then we shift the entire basis of much present-day instruction. We change the role of the teacher. It means, too, that we will then create a tremendous demand for new-type, multimedia libraries, sometimes called instructional materials centers. We shall need more short films, more recordings, more filmstrips, more paperbacks, more reference works for use in individualized instruction.

If the shift to asking questions is accompanied by self-diagnostic and self-instructional materials and the use of new types of examination, then the present lockstep of time spent in college or professional schools can be broken up. The rigid four years of high school and the inflexible four years of college may become a formless ritual. Mastering planned and unplanned learning, rather than time spent, becomes the basic control mechanism.

When time is so precious in one's learning career, why hasn't there been more concern with ways to shorten (or sometimes lengthen) the four-year college program? There are obvious ways to do it, one being to attend college for three years without the typical three-month summer vacation. Advanced placement examinations can also be used. The great values of correspondence instruction have not been sufficiently probed. The studies of Sidney Pressey and Marie Flesher have shown the possibilities of reduction of time spent in college. Today, with modern methods of mediating instruction, the curriculum should fit the learner—not the other way round.

The higher literacy in which we emphasize independence of learning requires a sharp increase in the quality of our instruments of evaluation. I visualize a situation where a person can go to a computer with a printed test and take an examination on almost any subject under the sun. It might be on his proficiency in a foreign language, on his ability to pass a test to get on the police force, on the quality of his logical thinking, and so on. The nationwide vocabulary testing which we have been doing at The Ohio State University could easily be handled by a computer, which would then record the progress of anyone who takes the tests.

What progress has been made in teaching critical

reading, critical listening, critical observing? One of my tasks in the Payne Fund studies of the thirties was to prepare a book for high school students, *How to Appreciate Motion Pictures,* which would help them judge the quality and meaning of motion pictures, to help them become discriminating viewers, in short, to become visually literate. Later I wrote another book, *How To Read a Newspaper,* aimed at developing critical newspaper readers. In my revision of the latter book I have also emphasized the critical viewing of television news. The higher literacy involves critical reading, listening, and observing. The lower literacy emphasizes the acquiring mind; the higher literacy develops the inquiring mind, a key goal of modern schools and colleges. The higher literacy, using new-type libraries, puts emphasis in school and college on learning to learn and developing a spirit of inquiry which motivates all learning.

Four years ago members of the reading staff at The Ohio State University completed a study on critical reading in grades one through six. I visited some of these classes when the experiment was under way and can testify to the fact that remarkable things occurred when the teachers emphasized the higher literacy in reading, set up clear-cut goals in thinking, and evaluated to see whether the goals were achieved. At the end of one class I asked a group of second-graders who had been studying the difference between folk tales and fables whether they read these stories to their parents or to brothers and sisters. Many of them did. When one boy said he didn't, I asked him to whom he read them.

"My St. Bernard dog," he replied.

"How many stories have you read him?"

"Twenty."

"How do you tell whether he likes a story?"

"He licks the pages."

"What story did he like best?"

"*How to Train a Dog.*"

We are likely to think that the higher literacy deals with the upper years of high school and college. Not so. The higher mental processes, those of reflective analysis and synthesis, occur at all levels. Note, for example, the inferences involved in these definitions given in interviews with inner-city first-grade children:

breeze - when the trees bow their heads; air out mouth

college - go to learn

mountain - what the bear walks over

rain - when clouds get together

scalp - under your hair

so - used all the time in arguing

true - news except weather reports

weather - a chart

nature - life or something

drown - in the river but he is not dead

dead - somebody buries you

pill - take pills when you don't want no more babies; vitamin

married - you're going to get involved

Or note these words, many of them created by eighth-grade students in inner-city Columbus schools:

benedictorial - kind, blessed

graphomatic - writes by itself

phonomatic - makes sounds by itself

retrometer - measures re-entry thrust

audict - likes to hear records

telematic - remote control

monocar - car on one rail

solarscope - sun viewer

disinject - take out

astrocraft - spaceship

barophone - measures weight by sound waves

telesonic - distant sounds

The great revolution in education will not come through technology, although it may be greatly aided by it. The revolution will come as we shift the role of both the teacher and the student. We have been input-minded. We think about the teacher, the book, the film, but we do not think about the output which the input is designed to produce.

Our schools and colleges are dominated by the lower mental processes—the reproduction of information instead of its production. We spend too much time acquiring information (a lower mental process) and too little time producing or creating knowledge, using knowledge (a higher mental process). We emphasize the duplication of knowledge but do too little with creative explication, implication, and application.

Accepting a choice made for us is a lower mental process. But the assessment of choices, setting up and developing priorities to meet varying situations, is a higher mental process. We will not educate unless we let students bear the consequences, good and bad, of their own decision-making. It is well to remember in these revolutionary times that hate and love both draw compound interest.

A person who tries to live the examined life pays his debts to the past by assuming new obligations to the future. We cannot directly pay the debt of gratitude which we owe Socrates, but we can avoid living "the unexamined life." Jefferson is gone, but we can still swear "eternal hostility against every form of tyranny over the mind of man." We can remember with Tom Paine that "the harder the conflict, the more glorious the triumph." Or with Henry L. Stimson that "the great sin is cynicism."

The socially illiterate man takes the short view; the socially literate man takes the long view. The short view is illustrated in a fable by the Russian poet Krylov about a pig who ate his fill of acorns under an oak tree and started to root around the tree. A crow sitting in the oak tree remarked, "You should not do this. If you lay bare the roots, the tree will wither and die." "Let it die," replied the pig. "Who cares as long as there are acorns?"

The long view, the one of planting unseen harvests, is illustrated by Marshal Lyautey, who, when he was in Africa, asked his gardener to obtain and plant a certain tree. The gardener replied that this tree did not reach maturity for two hundred years. The Marshal replied, "In that case there's no time to lose. Plant it this afternoon."

What we must strive for unceasingly is the higher literacy that enlightens, that causes us to think about and to concern ourselves with the condition of man. Aeschylus was the favorite poet of Robert Kennedy, and here is what Kennedy told a group of Negroes in a parking lot in Indianapolis on the cold, bitter night when Martin Luther King was slain: "Let us dedicate ourselves to what the Greeks wrote so many years ago, to tame the savageness of man and make gentle the life of the world."

A call for serious, informed controversy on critical problems does not mean that we should butt our heads against a stone wall when we ought better walk around it. But if there are no major controversies gripping the attention of a school, a college, or a business, then that institution is dying—training for the past, not educating for the future. Serious, sustained discussion on these controversies reveals whether we are dealing with a man-size issue or with a piddling enterprise unworthy of anyone's important time and thought.—Edgar Dale, "Good Reasons for Doing Nothing," *The News Letter,* Vol. XXVI, No. 3, December 1960.

Educational Evaluation in the Revolutionary Age

Ralph W. Tyler

Educational evaluation, as with every major phase of education, is meeting new demands in this revolutionary age. Since one omnibus volume on new roles and new means of evaluation was published in 1969,[1] and another expounding a very comprehensive conception of the field is being prepared by a committee of Phi Delta Kappa headed by Egon Guba and Dan Stufflebeam, it is not necessary for me to attempt inclusiveness in my presentation here. In fact, I do not have the breadth and depth required for this task. I have chosen, instead, to examine certain facets of current developments that seem to me particularly important at this time.

Profound transformations are taking place today in conceptions of educational evaluation, and some

Ralph W. Tyler is director emeritus of the Center for Advanced Study in the Behavioral Sciences.

significant new practices are beginning to emerge. Both are responses to new educational problems arising from the so-called contemporary social revolution. Since the close of World War II, the rising aspirations of oppressed peoples have created scores of new nations and thousands of new educational institutions throughout the world. In the United States, the civil rights movement has awakened new hopes for material, political and social advancement on the part of minority groups that previously gave little or no voice to their concerns for the limited educational opportunities furnished by American schools and colleges.

At first, the massive blocks to the educational achievements of minorities were perceived as due almost wholly to restrictions in the admissions process, and gross inequalities in the provision of teachers, facilities and supplies to those handicapped by poverty and racial and ethnic discrimination in comparison with other children and youth. No widespread improvement in the educational achievements of the disadvantaged, however, came with the increasing adoption of public policies aimed at the equalization of educational opportunities and with the provision of federal funds to aid the education of disadvantaged children under Title I of the Elementary and Secondary Education Act of 1965. By 1970, the problem of responding constructively to these higher aspirations seemed more complex and difficult than had been apparent 10 years earlier. It is becoming clear that the historic conceptions and procedures of American schools and colleges are not appropriate for stimulating, guiding and appraising the learning of children and youth who have difficulties in their school work.

Schools and Colleges as Sorting Institutions

Why do many children fail to learn in school when they are quick to acquire new behavior patterns on the playground, at home, or on the street? The same children who give up after a few minutes of work on school assignments can be seen practicing baseball or a new dance step for hours at a time. Every child who has no serious physical handicap is capable of learning the kinds of behavior emphasized by schools and colleges. Why are 15 to 25 per cent of our children failing to attain the level of literacy required to hold skilled jobs?

The establishment of schools took place before the industrial revolution and of course long before the emergence of our present, post-industrial society. When most people are unskilled laborers, only a few are needed for the occupational, social, and political elite. Schools, in the past, have been more largely sorting and selecting agents than educational ones. Grades, examinations and tests have been employed to sort children and youth for courses, curricular tracks, admission to college, and the like. Although school officials and teachers have largely been unconscious of it, the curriculum itself, with its focus on middle-class illustrations, its assumptions regarding the backgrounds of children when they start to school, its pacing, its opportunities for pupil practice, and its reward system, has also been a major sorting instrument. This mechanism has been effective in limiting the number of qualified applicants to college to correspond roughly to the openings available to them on graduation in business, industrial and political leadership, in the professions, and in the upper social strata.

When I was in elementary school, more than half my classmates dropped out before graduating from the eighth grade. They were able to get jobs on the farms and in other unskilled or semi-skilled occupations. Only 10 per cent of my age mates graduated from high school, the others dropping out along the line to obtain employment or to help at home. Only three per cent went on to college.

In the contemporary post-industrial society that characterizes the United States, only five per cent of the labor force is unskilled. Opportunities for employment in technical, professional, managerial and service occupations have increased more than 300 per cent in one generation. While the uneducated and untrained comprise an alarming percentage of "hard core unemployed," demands are increasing for doctors, nurses and health personnel generally, for teachers, supervisors and others in education, for many kinds of workers in the social services and in the field of recreation, for accountants, administrators, engineers and scientists. In civic life the need is great for citizens who are knowledgeable about our many serious domestic and international problems and who can examine alternative solutions objectively.

As the importance of the family in a society where other primary institutions have lost much of their potency is being recognized, the need for parents who understand the functions of child-rearing and are able to develop a strong family setting for its members is increasingly expressed. Furthermore, the potential for individual self-realization offered by the variety of arts and indoor and outdoor recreational developments is now seen as heavily dependent upon an education that is humanistic in the best sense of the word. Our society is now seeking to identify potential talents of many sorts and to furnish opportunities for these talents to be actualized through education. Schools are no longer accepted as adequate if they operate primarily to sort students.

Currently schools are expected to educate all their pupils; yet most are bound to a system in which all learners are expected to move at the same rate and those performing less satisfactorily than others are discouraged and give up or get farther and farther behind so that they lack the earlier achievement required to perform the later learning tasks.

We know enough about the way in which complex behavior is learned to realize that the learner is aided by starting with behavior he can readily acquire, and after he masters the first step he moves on step by step. He masters each new step if it is largely based on the preceding one. Complex behavior is acquired through a sequence of steps. An adept learner works out his own sequence, but many children need help, and for them it is necessary to devise an effective learning sequence.

Placement and Mastery Tests

The pressure of minority groups on the schools to educate their children is slowly meeting response. The delay has been due to the fact that the old system has worked quite well with a majority of children so that it has not been questioned but rather we have talked about "slow learners" or "dull students." Now we are recognizing the need to reconstruct the learning system if we are to reach effectively the children who have not been learning previously. In the new systems, behavioral objectives, arranged in sequence, are being formulated and learning experiences selected or devised to enable students to attain these objectives in step-by-step progression. Such a system can be used in group instruction as well as in individual tutoring.

A teacher who tries to manage a learning system where every child is engaged in activities that he can perform finds two evaluation instruments of great help.[2] Since such a system requires the arrangement of learning experiences in sequence for each of the major objectives, and since children differ in the extent of their previous learning, for each student a decision must be made regarding a place in the sequence where he can begin. This decision is aided by a placement procedure or test that indicates what the student has already learned and what next step in the sequence he can expect to carry on successfully. After he has engaged in the learning activities designed for the step where he begins, a mastery test can furnish evidence that he has acquired the desired behavior and is ready to proceed with the next step in the sequence.

Current, widely-used achievement tests do not provide dependable information either for placement or for mastery purposes. They have been designed to measure individual differences among students, not to indicate where each one is on a learning sequence, or whether he has gained mastery of the step on which he has been working. The items used in achievement tests in a given subject are designed to sample the knowledge and skills commonly emphasized in the subject over several school grades. On the basis of tryouts, items are selected which are answered correctly by a greater percentage of children in each higher grade; for example, a greater per cent of fifth-grade children than fourth-grade children. Items are rejected that are answered correctly by most of the pupils or by few of them, since they do not discriminate among the pupils and thus do not serve to arrange them in order from those who get high scores to those who receive low ones. The result of this selection procedure is a test which does not reliably sample each objective and each step in a sequence.

A placement procedure useful for a teacher and the students in a learning system designed to help every child progress involves a two-step appraisal. The first is a test constructed to sample each major section of the learning sequence. A primary reading program, for example, may have a sequence in which the first several steps involve the use of simple oral communication, the second several steps are concerned with the alphabet, and the third, with the decoding of common phonemes. The first placement test would be constructed to sample reliably each of the three series of steps but would not furnish a reliable sample of the behavior in each step. It would provide, thereby, an indication of the major divisions in the sequence already learned and in what division the beginning step would be found. This enables the pupil to check himself on mastery tests within this division to identify the next step that he has not yet mastered.

When the pupil has carried through successfully the learning experiences which have been designed to enable him to acquire the behavior involved in this step, a mastery test furnishes new situations in which he can demonstrate his command of this behavior. A mastery test, hence, is quite different from current achievement tests. In the first place, it is based on the behavior to be learned in a sequential step in the learning system. There are as many mastery tests needed as there are steps in the sequence employed. The complexity and/or difficulty of the behavior sampled by a mastery test is determined by the complexity and/or difficulty of this behavior as it is to be used by the student as soon as he has mastered the step. For most school programs, the behavior learned in step 1 will then be used in step 2, and the behavior in step

2 will be used in step 3, and so on. This means that the requirement is for the student to be able to use in the next step the behavior he is learning in this step. This becomes the so-called "criterion referenced norm." At the points in the sequence where the behavior is primarily to be used outside the schoolroom or in other school subjects, the complexity and/or difficulty level commonly required become the "criterion referenced norms." This is another way of saying that a pupil has mastered the behavior when he is able to employ it successfully in the next stage of his life.

Note that mastery tests are not designed to spread out a distribution of pupils. Much of the effort of the teacher and the pupils is to learn something and be able to use it, not primarily to say that one is at the 90th, 60th, 40th or some other percentile in the distribution of pupils' scores on an achievement test. It is becoming clear that disadvantaged children can learn what schools seek to teach if systems are designed to facilitate learning rather than to sort children and to discourage those who do not learn easily on their own. Such a system requires new evaluation procedures, chief among which are placement and mastery tests.

The Census of Educational Achievement

Although minority groups are becoming most articulate in their concern for more and better education of their children, the American public generally is seeking more information about the educational effectiveness of the schools, and is raising seriously the question of the school's accountability for its efforts. Because education has become the servant of all our purposes, its effectiveness is of general public concern.

The educational tasks now faced require many more resources than have thus far been available, and they must be wisely used to produce the maximum results. To make these decisions, dependable information about the progress of education is essential. Otherwise, we scatter our efforts too widely and fail to achieve our goals. Yet, we do not now have the necessary comprehensive and dependable data.

We have reports on numbers of schools, buildings, teachers and pupils, and about the money expended, but we do not have sound and adequate information on educational results. Because dependable data are not available, personal views, distorted reports and journalistic impressions are the sources of public opinion, and the schools are frequently attacked and frequently defended without having necessary evidence to support either claim. This situation can be corrected only by a careful, consistent effort to obtain valid data to provide sound evidence about the purposes of American education. This is the purpose of the National Assessment of Educational Progress.

Because the purpose of the assessment is to provide helpful information about the progress of education which can be understood and accepted by public-spirited lay citizens, some new procedures were followed. In each field, scholars, teachers, and curriculum specialists formulated statements on the objectives which they believe faithfully reflect the contributions of the field and which the schools are seriously seeking to attain. For each of these major objectives, prototype exercises were constructed which, in the opinion of scholars and teachers, give students an opportunity to demonstrate the behavior implied by the objective. These lists of objectives, and prototype exercises which help to define them, were reviewed by a series of panels of public-spirited citizens living in various parts of the country in cities, towns, and rural areas. Each panel spent two days reviewing the material and making a judgment about each objective in terms of the questions: "Is this something important for people to learn today? Is it something I would like to have my children learn?" This process resulted in some revisions of the original listing of objectives, and some eliminations.

The procedure was designed to insure that every objective being assessed is: (1) considered important by scholars, (2) accepted as an educational task by the school, and (3) deemed desirable by leading lay citizens. This should help to eliminate the criticism frequently encountered with current tests in which some item is attacked by the scholar as representing shoddy scholarship or criticized by school people as something not in the curriculum, or by prominent laymen as being unimportant or technical trivia.

The fact that populations are to be assessed and not individuals makes it possible to extend the sampling of exercises far beyond that of any individual test in which each person takes it all. The first year's assessment, which included science, writing, and citizenship, required so many exercises that it would take one person 14 hours to complete the set. With a population sample, 14 persons each spending an hour were able to take all the exercises. This made the process a practicable one.

The assessment included both group exercises and individual ones. They were not limited to the usual test items. Interviews and observational procedures were also employed to learn more of interests, habits, and practices that have been learned. Since school objectives commonly include these areas, it is necessary to see that some assessment is made of these several kinds of attainment.

The National Assessment reports separately for populations within the total country, which vary among themselves and thus present different degrees and kinds of progress and different problems to be solved. Currently a probability sample is used for each of 256 populations defined by the following subdivisions: boys and girls, four geographic regions, four age groups (nine, thirteen, seventeen and young adult), four types of communities (large cities, small cities, suburban areas and rural), and two socioeconomic levels.

Educational Auditing

The National Assessment of Educational Progress will furnish useful information on the educational achievements of important population groups in the nation, but it will not satisfy local demands for dependable information about the learning of various groups of children and youth in the local schools. Organizations of blacks, of Puerto Ricans, and of Mexican Americans are proclaiming their beliefs that their children are not learning much of importance in the schools, and they are demanding evidence of the effectiveness of the schools in educating their children. The current widely-used achievement tests do not furnish the information demanded because they do not sample reliably the learning of those who are not near the average of the students. The scores are indications of where the students are placed in a distribution but do not report to parents what the students have learned.

In some cities the school administration has lost credibility so that some groups do not trust the reports that are released by school officials. As with the reporting of financial matters, there are increasing demands for independent educational audits. In one city, a large contract was awarded by the school system to an independent research organization to conduct an appraisal of the educational results of a new program instituted in schools which were under attack for failing to educate the children of minorities. Several organizations are now planning to provide independent educational auditing services.

In many respects an independent educational audit is similar to the National Assessment. The school or community awarding the contract will need to specify the objectives to be appraised, the geographic areas to be included, the ages or grades from which population samples are to be drawn and the kinds of professional review to be used. This is to assure validity and reliability in the construction and selection of assessment exercises, and in the design and conduct of the actual appraisal. The contractors will need to follow procedures in constructing or selecting assessment exercises which are similar to those used in the National Assessment. The fact that the audit usually will involve only a limited geographic region makes the sampling procedure simpler. Either the school or the home becomes the primary sampling unit. As with the National Assessment, no one pupil would be asked to take all the exercises, so that time required of any child or youth would be limited, even though the complete assessment involved several objectives for each subject and sampled achievement at several levels of performance.

A skeptical public would probably consider an independent audit one in which the outside contractor selects the persons to be tested, without the pupils or the school personnel knowing in advance who would be responding to what kinds of exercises. The outside contractor would also be responsible for keeping all exercises secure until after they had been administered by an agent of the contractor. The contractor would analyze and report the results. As with the National Assessment, a considerable number of the exercises used would be presented in the report, together with the percentage of the respondents who did the exercises successfully. The interested public could in this way get a clearer notion of what the schools are trying to teach and what success they are having. The independence of the audit might serve to restore greater credibility to the reports prepared by school officials.

Evaluating New Educational Programs

The experience with educational innovations during the Great Depression taught many of us that the decision to design or adopt a new educational program does not necessarily mean that a new program will actually be put into operation. In the Eight-Year Study which began in 1933, the year 1936 is probably the time at which a majority of the 30 school systems were operating programs that approximated the outlines of the plans submitted in 1932. In the Activity School Experiment in New York City, six years after it began, nearly 40 per cent of the classrooms of the "Activity Schools" were undistinguishable from the typical classrooms in other schools. We learned that the development of an operating program for an innovative plan is in itself a hard and time-consuming task. School administrators and teachers are not accustomed to system planning so that many necessary steps are not foreseen, but even more difficult is the translation of an idea into the actual habits, attitudes, understanding and skills required for effective implementation of the idea.

Although this lesson was learned by many who were involved in innovations in the 1930's, it has not been fully appreciated today. Title III programs, Title I programs, and other efforts at innovation have been adopted, and results have often been appraised a short time later without careful examination of the actual operational characteristics of the programs. Goodlad and his colleagues sampled the classroom practices of schools which were using the "new science curricula" developed with the support of the National Science Foundation. They found that almost 70 per cent of the classes were treating the new science course material as content to be memorized, whereas the basic principle on which the courses were devised was that of student inquiry.

The common evaluation design has overlooked the appraisal of the extent to which the objectives and the principles of the program plan are actually in operation. Such an appraisal can guide the implementation of the innovation, a process which is now very difficult because it does involve changes in subtle as well as easily handled procedures. Provus has elaborated a procedure for this stage of evaluation in his monograph, *A Discrepancy Model,* and has described it more briefly in his chapter in the 1969 Yearbook of the National Society for the Study of Education. He emphasizes the importance of viewing this as a way of identifying discrepancies between plans and operations and then to reconcile the two, not by assuming that either plans or operations are immutable, but rather to inquire, in connection with each discrepancy, how it is likely to affect the program and what modification of plan or operations or both will appear to improve the program.

When the operating program begins to perform in a way consistent with the revised plans, an evaluation of the effects of the new program should then be undertaken. For this purpose, evaluation instruments must be selected or devised that are appropriate for appraising the students' attainment of the objectives for which the program has been designed and also to assess possible unplanned effects, the so-called "side effects," as the term is used in medicine.

The features that are now being given more attention than in earlier efforts at evaluation are (1) the focus of the evaluation instruments on the particular learning objectives to see that the instruments are appropriate for the kinds of students involved and their stages of learning, (2) the development of appraisal procedures to assess the unplanned, sometimes negative effects, and (3) the study of the transfer of learning, that is the extent to which students are using outside school the concepts, the skills and the values they are learning in school. The purpose of education is not simply to develop a pupil who behaves effectively within the school, but to develop a person who has acquired and uses ways of thinking, feeling and acting that are relevant to a wide range of human experience. Part of the evaluation of an educational program involves sampling the out-of-school situations to find out how well his learning in the classroom is serving him in the home, on the playground, at work, and in other community settings.

Appraising Scholastic Aptitude

Assessing the educability of students has previously meant the administration of examinations called Scholastic Aptitude Tests. This area is now in controversy and confusion. The question of inherent educational potential can never be answered in precise terms since inherent potential cannot be assessed directly. Evidence on this question is restricted to studies of biological, particularly neurological, structures and functions on the one hand, and the outcome of educational efforts on the other. The confusion is also intensified by the failure to distinguish between questions that relate to the potential of an individual or a group of individuals to learn something, and those that relate to the differential learning rates or outcomes between individuals or groups. That is to say, evidence that a given individual or group learns something more rapidly than others on the average, or in a given time attains a higher average level of performance than another individual or group is often treated as though the evidence indicated that one individual or group could learn something and the other could not.

Learning is so characteristic of human individuals that one who fails to learn to acquire new patterns of behavior as he grows up is considered highly abnormal. From the standpoint of neural functioning, learning to use one's native language is about as demanding as any learning requirement of schools and colleges. To express an idea, one must draw upon extensive memory of words, must pattern the sentence structure in a way that is appropriate for the kind of meaning to be conveyed, and must utilize a particular appropriate inflection from a number of possibilities. Comprehension of what someone is saying is also complex in neurological functioning since the ambiguity of the alternative meanings of words and of sentence structures usually cannot be resolved until the entire sentence has been spoken. Since the vast majority of humans learn to use their native language, it appears probable that most human beings are inherently capable of learning complex behavior.

Another source of evidence is obtained from

experiments in which efforts are made to teach deprived or otherwise handicapped individuals. The results are usually positive although the research reports often state that different individuals require different approaches to learning. Differences are also reported in the rates of learning and the accuracy of discrimination in transferring from the learning situation to other situations in which the learning could be applied. It seems safe to conclude that we face no serious problem in finding many more youth who are capable of learning what schools and colleges seek to teach.

The evaluation of educability really involves identifying a wide range of developing talents and abilities on which school learning can be built or in connection with which new learning can be stimulated. The aspect of evaluation helpful in dealing with educability is to assess the effectiveness of the school or college learning environment. Learning in school is not simply a matter of the ability of the child or youth but also of the adequacy and appropriateness of the school environment. Beginning with the work of Sheviakov in the Eight Year Study, and extended and refined by Stern, Stein, Bloom and Pace, the assessment of the school or college learning environment has become a practicable procedure which can be related to the increasingly comprehensive appraisal of the individual's intellectual skills, interests, and significant previous experiences. Now we are better able to talk about the probability of educating an individual in a particular school situation. This is a great step forward from the older intelligence or scholastic aptitude conceptions and procedures.

For more than half a century, achievement test construction has largely been conceived as the building of tests that will measure individual differences among students on characteristics assumed to be unidimensional. Scores have been obtained by making assumptions about the distribution of learned behavior among students. Results have been reported in terms of relative norms, not in terms of the behavior students have acquired. These conceptions, procedures, and devices are not adequate to meet a number of the current pressing demands. Students of evaluation are now formulating new conceptions, working out new procedures, and beginning to construct new instruments. These efforts are essential if educational evaluation is to serve the revolutionary age.

NOTES

1. National Society for the Study of Education, *Educational Evaluation: New Roles, New Means*, 68th Yearbook, Part II. Distributed by the University of Chicago Press, 1969.
2. Lindvall and Cox describe the use of more than two tests in their chapter on the Evaluation of Individual Instruction in *Educational Evaluation: New Roles, New Means.*

Curriculum Planning for the Revolutionary Age

John I. Goodlad

Given the title assigned to me, "Curriculum Planning for the Revolutionary Age," it is a temptation to deal with the electronic school of the future in which human and machine teachers and their students must learn to live together. For reasons which presumably will come clear as I proceed, I shall resist this topic and deal with two much less glamorous themes and their relationships. The first pertains to the current impotence of the school. The second theme is the accountability which all of us share in the necessary process of reconstructing the school.

One of many sobering realizations of our time is that the curriculum, at all levels of the formal educational structure, is characterized by a pervasive impotence. It frequently is described as irrelevant and as not "gripping" the students. Close examination reveals,

John I. Goodlad is dean of the Graduate School of Education, University of California, Los Angeles.

however, that many of the topics and ideas are indeed relevant. They simply do not "come on strong." In the long and involved process from conceptualization for the curriculum to inclusion in it, the great ideas, issues, and methods of men somehow lose their power, ultimately arriving limp and inert before the student. There is need for change—not tinkering, but sweeping change.

With each passing day we see more clearly the trenchant meaning of one of John Gardner's many significant statements on change. He said, in effect, that our central problem today is not merely adjusting to and coping with change or even just effecting change, important though all these may be. It is, rather, that of reconstructing our social institutions and managing constructive change in the face of the ever-present dangers of social disintegration on one hand and bureaucratization on the other. Maintaining productive disequilibrium during an era of social revolution demands individual stamina and self-discipline of a kind that always is in short supply.

We are, once more, at a time in history when the forces of change appear to pull more against than with each other. This certainly is so at present with our educational system. There is growing disillusionment with our schools. There has been disillusionment before. This time, however, there is much less confidence that we need only to do better what we have tried to do before. Some say in despair that the school has outlived its usefulness, and should be abolished.

At the very time when we desperately need clarity, the matter of who should make what educational decisions is exceedingly confused. State legislators pass laws which, as often as not, restrict teachers in their efforts to adapt method and content to the needs of learners. State and local boards of education frequently duplicate each other and, at times, assume authority presumably delegated to administrators. Superintendents, principals, and teachers are not at all clear on their realms of jurisdiction. Likewise, the lay citizen knows not how to influence the schools or to participate meaningfully in their improvement. The forces which must collaborate if the schools are to be improved rarely communicate, let alone work together.

It is not at all uncommon, in the midst of complex problems and social disarray, for simple answers couched in slogans to emerge. One of many current slogans is "accountability." Clearly, in the eyes of many, teachers are responsible for children's learning and must be held accountable for improvement. Ironically, the call for accountability often is accompanied by restrictions on the very freedoms teachers need if they are to be held accountable. It should not surprise us, then, to find that increasing teacher militancy is accompanied not only be demands for higher salaries but also by requests for improved working conditions, including a larger say in educational decisions.

One cannot legitimately quarrel with legislators who seek to improve education through the passage of better legislation, with school board members who enter zealously into their responsibilities, with citizens who desire to act for better schools, and with teachers who want freedom to teach. All these groups, in their zeal or in their less commendable drive for power, tend to reach beyond the land that is rightfully theirs to plow, to neglect their own ill-kept furrows. Schools and the children in them are, as a consequence, the losers.

Let me now explore in some depth the charge of the school's impotence and the matter of confusion in regard to who should make what educational decisions. My thesis is that the two are closely related.

Educational change and innovation presumably were characteristic of the decade in American education beginning in the late 1950's and concluding in the late 1960's. During much of this decade, I had the good fortune to participate in nationwide studies which took me into a great many schools. As I visited, I became increasingly uneasy; the changes then being talked about seemed not to be finding their way into school and classroom. It was as though there was one level of education at which exciting ideas were discussed, but another—the level for which these ideas were intended—that seemed not to be enjoying their benign influence.

With this discrepancy formulated as a working hypothesis, I selected ten colleagues from the University Elementary School at UCLA, with a view to taking a more careful look at elementary schools in the United States. A second group under my direction subsequently looked at selected elementary and secondary schools in California. A report of the first set of visits to 150 classrooms in 67 schools is now available: *Behind the Classroom Door,* by John I. Goodlad, M. Frances Klein, and Associates (Worthington, Ohio: Charles A. Jones Publishing Company, 1970). In seeking to organize the information from thousands of pages of anecdotal data, we were guided by a set of what we called "reasonable expectations" for our schools—that is, expectations for what would be reasonable to find in our schools if some of the most frequently recommended improvements were now, in large measure, implemented. Some of these recommended improvements go back to the turn of the century; some of them are much more recent. It is difficult to conceive of educators not having been rather generously exposed to them.

Of these reasonable expectations, some pertained rather directly to the curriculum. First, given the amount of attention to defining educational objectives, going back several decades, it would be reasonable to assume that teachers, singly and collectively, would have rather clear-cut perceptions of what they were trying to do. Second, it seemed reasonable to assume that there would be considerable emphasis on "learning how to learn" rather than covering assorted collections of subject matter. Third, since this is, presumably, "the golden age of instructional materials," it seemed reasonable to assume that a wide range of such materials would be visibly in use. Fourth, given attention to individual differences among learners, it also seemed reasonable to assume that many different kinds of learning activities would be under way at any time, being pursued individually or in groups. Fifth, since virtually all the newer approaches to curriculum have stressed inductive discovery methods, it seemed reasonable to expect that these would be in evidence in the classroom.

This abbreviated list of expectations will suffice to make the central point: there was an enormous gap between our "reasonable expectations" and what we found in the classrooms visited. It was very difficult to determine, during observation of teachers, just what they were endeavoring to accomplish at any given time. The pattern of rewards for children's performance provided few dependable clues. There was very little stress on "learning how to learn" but a great deal on covering specific content laid out for the grade. Instead of a wide range of instructional materials being used, emphasis was on the textbook, sometimes to the exclusion of all else.

Most classes proceeded as a group, with relatively little or no provision for individual differences in the learning rate of students. Primary classes were divided into three groups for reading, for example, but the children in any given group used the same books, often in rote fashion. Rather than there being appropriate opportunity for the student to learn inductively, telling and questioning by the teacher proved to be the prime method of instruction. The findings in our sample of classes were surprisingly uniform, whether the school was an inner-city one, enrolling many disadvantaged children, or whether the school was considered to be more innovative than was customary for the district.

In addition, we found only a handful of schools in which the faculties were at work on the central problems which teachers and principals identified for us. Although many teachers were busy at inservice education activities, few appeared to be involved with these school problems. Teachers were at work on their individual interests, seldom coming together as a total group to engage in serious consideration of the school's goals and priorities. Perhaps as a consequence, the schools we visited appeared to lack a sense of purpose or a personality expressing the collective interests of their inhabitants.

A little reflection reveals that schooling is probably the largest industry in this country that does not provide for the systematic updating of its personnel at the cost of this industry. Lacking in job specifications and in an analysis of need in relation to changing jobs, schools and teachers probably fit each others' needs only as a very rough approximation. The tasks of teaching and managing the schools are not clearly defined; responsibility for defining them has not been assigned;

and, it is exceedingly difficult to know just who should be held accountable for what.

The impotence of the schools is not, clearly, the fictional creation of a few eloquent malcontents. Rather, this impotence appears to be pervasive. It will not go away in the relatively unobtrusive fashion of its coming. It will not be easily changed. If we are to have exciting, relevant schools for the revolutionary age, then little short of an educational revolution will suffice. A revolution that pits groups one against another will not suffice, either. It must be a revolution against a condition—a condition of petrification in the schools—a revolution within which each responsible group assumes its appropriate role.

Confused Roles

One could cite thousands of instances to illustrate the confusion—nay, chaos—with respect to authority and responsibility for decision-making in education. But just a few examples will suffice. They are *not* fictitious.

The board of a fast-growing school district approved construction of a modern, open-space school. The superintendent then picked a principal to design and implement the program for which the building presumably was designed. Within a year after the school was opened, several parents complained to the board about undue noise and freedom in the large open spaces being used for team teaching. The board reacted by instructing the superintendent to order the principal and his staff to revert to the more orderly procedures presumed to characterize traditional school buildings. The principal resisted, requesting and being granted opportunity to conduct a survey of parental opinion regarding the school. The returns were highly favorable. Soon after, the superintendent moved on to bigger things and the board selected this principal as the new superintendent. Cases of this kind seldom turn out so happily.

A second anecdote pertains to a public exchange between a newspaper staff writer and the board of a junior college district. The staff writer raised questions about the board's involvement in the management of the junior colleges under its jurisdiction, citing specifically, as an example, board actions on the professional travel of individual faculty members. The vice chairman of the board responded in a letter to the editor, claiming the appropriatenesses of such behavior on the part of the board and citing as reason the responsibility of the board for the management of tax money.

A state legislature, unhappy over the results of reading tests in the schools, proposed that at least half of all time devoted to the teaching of reading in the state should stress oral reading. As can be imagined, this proposal caused no small outcry on the part of primary teachers in the state.

For years, the sixth-grade class of an elementary school had studied the United Nations. Teachers, parents, and children came to expect this as standard fare for the first semester. On one ocassion, just before school was to open, the regular teacher became seriously ill and was granted a year's sick leave. The substitute who was hired had her own ideas about what should be taught in the sixth grade and proceeded to teach, during the first semester, a social studies unit dealing with exploring and governing outer space. Many parents and several of the teachers became quite upset and exerted pressure to discontinue the unit, attacking the new teacher in the process. The teacher soon came to the principal in desperation, wondering whether it would be advisable for her to resign.

A state board of education decreed that, henceforth, persons would be certified to teach in the state only if they held an undergraduate major, an undergraduate minor, and certain specified courses in education. The teacher-preparing institutions found that compliance with the new regulations virtually eliminated all courses in education other than those specified, and began to release or reassign, wherever possible, the surplus faculty members, most of whom taught certain specialized courses often lumped together as "methods courses." Within a few years of this succession of decisions, there was a growing outcry against the quality of teaching of reading in the schools of the state. Preparation in the teaching of reading had been seriously cut by the earlier decisions. Nonetheless, it was proposed statewide that teachers now be held accountable for improvement in the teaching of reading. Testing of children was to occur at regular intervals.

These anecdotes reveal many significant decisions by groups of persons who should be held responsible and accountable for various aspects of the educational process. Were the right decisions being made by the right people?

The education of a child in school is much more than the relatively simple matter of his interacting with the teacher and with the learning fare selected by that teacher. His school education is a product of many decisions by many people, not all of whom know him, his talents, his interests, and his needs. Many of the persons making these decisions have never questioned whether or not they should. Most have never met the others whose decisions affect the learner at the end of the line. Most are quite unaware of the ultimate impact of the decisions they make.

One result of this situation is duplication, overlap and confusion in the bundle of decisions for education which are made. The laws passed by state legislatures often hit their mark, but not always with beneficial consequences. Even the most permissive and helpful legislation frequently is confused and confounded by directives laid down by state departments of education. Local boards of education vacillate between assuming too much authority and responsibility for some spheres of involvement while completely neglecting others. Some superintendents virtually neglect their principals. Others require that principals appear in person before the school board to request permission on matters which should fall within their scope of independent judgment and authority.

Lack of clarity in matters of educational decision-making can and does create conflict. Teachers are instructed to use a phonics approach in teaching reading, but obviously, must risk violating such directives in dealing with children whose hearing is impaired. Principals and teachers in many schools violate the existing education code in order to exercise their own best judgment in dealing with educationally handicapped children. In some states and school districts, it is almost impossible to teach without violating requirements enacted at remote levels of decision-making.

Perhaps the most serious consequence of this confusion is that some of the most important educational decisions go by default. State boards of education, for example, frequently hassle over how reading should be taught—a matter for which they have no competence—while neglecting to give attention to the inadequate, outdated system of financing the schools which exists in most states. Many local boards stoutly resist any educational guidance from federal levels of education, especially in the area of determining what is to be accomplished in their schools. Very few school boards give systematic attention to this question. The ends and means they seek to protect are determined largely by those commercial publishing houses whose textbooks are adopted for their schools. Principals and teachers are quite capable of identifying a host of complex problems faced by their schools at any given time. Only a handful of school faculties, however, is at work on the problems which they themselves identify as pressing.

Into this situation of overlap, confusion, conflict and neglect enters the matter of accountability, usually couched in the rhetoric of teachers being held responsible for children's learning. But we are all responsible in some way for the condition of the schools and must be held accountable. Congress must be held responsible and accountable for placing at least a minimum floor of support under the schools of every state so that all children and youth have equal access to educational opportunity. State legislatures must be held responsible and accountable for redesigning our anachronistic structure for financing schools so that funds are adequately and equitably distributed for educational purposes. Administrators must be held responsible and accountable not only for distributing resources so that maximum educational benefits result but also for providing the planning framework within which the creative efforts of teachers and principal may flourish. Teachers must be held responsible and accountable for selecting methods and materials appropriate to the needs of individual learners. Local boards of education must be held responsible and accountable for assuring teachers the freedom and protection they need for designing tailor-made education for each child. The schools cannot be reconstructed when all those responsible for them are working at cross-purposes. The critical tasks of educational reform require for their accomplishment the collaborative effort of all groups within the framework of a reasonably rational plan of action.

Toward More Rational Educational Decisions

Two themes run through this paper. First, the schools are not sufficiently vital. Neither the curriculum nor teaching grips children and youth as it should. Second, the currently popular concept of accountability—usually applied only to teachers—must be extended to encompass all those groups currently or potentially responsible for determining the condition of our schools. The application of this much more comprehensive conception of accountability requires careful delineation of the full array of decisions to be made in the educational enterprise, and allocation of responsibility for making them. What is called for, then, is a much more rational approach to educational decision-making. But man is far from rational in the conduct of his affairs and, at times, even fears an excess of commitment to rationality. The possibility of our becoming overly rational in the conduct of educational affairs, however, is quite remote.

The foregoing implies that there are *appropriate* decisions to be made at federal, state and local levels of educational responsibility and *appropriate* decisions for professionals to make collectively and individually. The prime task for the nation is to determine the nature of the gap separating us from our best visions of where we might be as people, and our present condition. Such analysis must be followed by appropriate action. The Supreme Court Decision of 1954 on racial segregation in our schools is a superb illustration of federal responsibility. Basic principles pertaining to the rights of citizens in this country were being violated. As a beginning step toward more rapid elimination of discrimination, a law was passed. The law, of course, did not eliminate prejudice; this is a task for education. The making of such distinctions is imperative if appropriate means to the attainment of goals are to be used.

Responsible involvement of the federal government in educational matters requires that there be ongoing analysis of the education gap—that is, the gap between visions and realities, which might be closed effectively through educational means. In the ideal state, there must be free inquiry into what is required for the self-renewal of that state, free inquiry supported by the very government which stands to be criticized by the results of the inquiry it supports. This form of free inquiry seems never to be adequately supported and always to be threatened. One of the strengths of this nation in recent years has been the emergence of private philanthropy, supporting free inquiry on the part of observers and critics of the national scene. Such inquiry affects public policy. This is the very reason that it should be supported rather than restricted. It is imperative that we maintain centers of free inquiry supported from both private and public sources. Policy centers do not make the nation's decisions. They describe; they analyze; they project trends into the future; they recommend. It is then up to the government to see that goals and priorities are established. The federal government has the resources and must muster the will to provide special inducements for remedying past neglect and avoiding pitfalls lying ahead. One area of current neglect, for example, is development of the talents of our young people. Schools funnel human resources into a narrow range of expectation and approval. Developing talent requires a quite different conception of schooling, with school becoming a concept rather than a place. Either our children and youth must be released from the schoolhouse to study with the artists, musicians, writers, sculptors, scientists, physicians, and all the others who could be serving as models for the young, or these human models must be brought into the schoolhouse.

The state, similarly, must have mechanisms for the identification of priorities. Needed in each state is a human resources research center, such as that recently established for the province of Alberta, Canada. In the realm of education, such centers would be studying, for example, the relationship between financial allocation for education and projected needs. Following such studies, the legislature would be allocating more resources for junior colleges at one period in time and more resources for the education of specialists in the health sciences at another. Debating at the legislative level such matters as the relative merits of various approaches to the teaching of reading would be regarded as gross irresponsibility. But it would be appropriate for a state assembly or board of education to take cognizance of a report prepared by an educational policy center regarding inadequate understanding of the reading process and to recommend that research into the problem be placed on the priority listing of a national institute for education.

Local boards of education must choose among difficult alternatives in the light of national and state commitments and local needs. An influx of Spanish-speaking residents or a dramatic rise in the use of drugs among school-age children should call for the realignment of priorities and appropriate reallocation of funds. But when a school board finds itself hiring and firing teachers or passing upon approved pedagogical procedures, it is abrogating its prime responsibilities to take on inappropriate ones, and must be held accountable.

In a rational process of educational decision-making, boards of education interact with their superintendents in regard to the establishment and fulfillment of priority aims. The board of education holds the superintendent accountable for the attainment of goals to which they are jointly committed but permits and even encourages a great deal of flexibility in regard to the selection of means. When in doubt about the abilities or methods of the superintendent, they should seek independent, external counsel and, when convinced of the ineffectiveness of the man they have chosen, they should ask for his resignation, not restrict the freedom of an incumbent to select means for goal attainment. It would be the better part of wisdom, also, for the board subsequently to review its procedures for selecting its superintendent.

The superintendent, in turn, must hold his principals accountable for developing processes by means of which each school will become a vital force in its community. The superintendent does not set the goals for each school, but he does monitor the process, assuring himself that each faculty is establishing priorities which, in turn, bear a contributing relationship to the goals accepted for the district. Finally, the principal holds each teacher accountable for determination and attainment of specific objectives related directly to priorities for the school. In a rational system, principals do not impose pedagogical techniques on their teachers. But they do endeavor to provide a structure within which pedagogical skills may be updated. Teachers are held accountable, however, not for adherence to prescribed means but for progress toward the attainment of established objectives.

It is clear that the task of delineating appropriate authority and responsibility for educational decision-making is scarcely begun. While this is a serious problem, it is not nearly so serious as the fact that there currently is no provision in our educational superstructure for assuring that it will be accomplished. If we are to have vital curricula for the revolutionary age, the first step is to sort out of present confusion and neglect some preliminary designations of what appears to be appropriate responsibility for all the participating groups. This in itself would justify a curriculum policy center, perhaps as part of the proposed National Institute for Education.

But no system will work unless the humans in it *assume* their appropriate responsibility. Each group has a further responsibility to mankind: to resist all those who, out of innocence, ignorance, or ill intentions, would usurp its authority. A classic instance of assuming appropriate responsibility on one hand and resisting the usurpation of authority on the other is attributed to Robert Maynard Hutchins during his tenure as president of the University of Chicago. It is reported that a member of the board of trustees suggested to his colleagues at the beginning of a meeting that the political activities of Professor Y. be discussed. President Hutchins immediately rose and stated, "Gentlemen, to discuss the activities of Professor Y. is to discuss my resignation."

Commentary

John M. Brewer

As an educator who has spent almost all of his professional career in schools that are located in areas of blight and slums, I'm afraid I do not see those essential curriculum changes, described by Dr. Goodlad, coming either fast or fundamentally enough to save the scene for educationally disadvantaged children.

There is substantial evidence that big city educators are being challenged by a whole generation of young people—black and white—who compose an inner-city culture of poverty. They are insistently demanding that their education be relevant, meaningful, and significant to their lives and that the curriculum should not be a tool of a suburban culture of affluence. Their challenge to us must not be ignored, evaded, or put down.

There are several points of reference that I feel provide a seedbed for creative thinking in any attempt to deal with revolutionary curriculum changes amid the turbulence of the 1970's. A great deal of effort has gone into curriculum revision, yet the dreary picture persists of excessive dropout rates, absenteeism, discontent, and functional illiteracy even after twelve years of so-called education. The demand today is for a new breed of administrators, persons who are willing to lead the accountability parade.

The first thing that we have to come to grips with is: What is the price? Perhaps the price is survival. If we are going to come to grips with the issues of great weight and moment, there must be open-ended communication. That leads to the challenge of models. In essence, there is an underlying theme here, and that is to break with tradition. Once we feel that this is a road that we may want to travel, I think that we have to engage in some sort of self-examination.

John M. Brewer is the assistant superintendent for school-community affairs, Pittsburgh Public Schools.

In dealing with the problem of price, I think we have to deal also with the realities of the massive failures of some of our education. As I move out into the community, I hear the human cry, particularly of the minority groups. They say, "We want control of our schools." And we rear back and start, having great concerns about their ability to deal with the curriculum. We begin to rationalize, and actually we are coming out in an irrational posture. Poor people often have a way of telling it how it is. They say: "Hey, man, you're all messed up—and give us a chance to mess up too." As I see it, the price is that we have to come to grips with the degree or the level of community involvement. We have to take a position, a relevancy position, on the thrust for community control. This is curriculum, too.

Then we ask, "How much is in our reach?" and we look at our resources. They're either stagnant or they're elusive, and then we get hung-up again. I have never heard a definition of quality education for an educationally disadvantaged child that makes sense. It's all a bunch of rhetoric. If you don't believe it, read the rhetoric, then try to put it into something tangible or manageable—and see the academic experiences of kids first. We fool around with "quality education," but we deal very little with equality of results.

A second question relative to Dr. Goodlad's remarks is: What are the crisis areas that affect this curriculum in a revolutionary age? Now we have to deal with this. We can't run away from it today as we did yesterday. If you don't believe this, go into the inner city. How do we deal with polarization and its many ramifications? How do we deal with the conflict and the controversies that surface and spill over into the schools and find their way into the curriculum? And how will this serve as a change agent, or how will schools respond to and wrestle with this particular problem?

Social break-up today must be dealt with within the structure of the curriculum, whether it is political upheaval or whether it's due to the numerous factions that have surfaced because of the periods of crisis or (to reverse myself) periods of pre-crisis, crisis, and post-crisis. These crises seem to numb and paralyze educators from coast to coast, particularly when they have to deal with problems of decentralization and the very sticky and sensitive problems of desegregation. How do we really pump the lifeblood into that one massive problem we're facing, which is basically integration? How do we deal with the realities of Black Power? How do we accept or take a position in terms of the anxiety, the frustration, the alienation, and the hasty retreat that are now surfacing in our schools. And how do we take a position in terms of minority groups who say, "Well, let's forget curriculum in the total context of society and let's do our thing?" I think that the most challenging and threatening question which has to be answered in respect to the exciting ideas and recommendations of Dr. Goodlad is: How do we honestly process the heterogeneous inputs that inhibit but nevertheless get fed into the decision-making processes, the planning, the implementation, and the policy affecting curriculum for a revolutionary age?

I have saved the most controversial question until last: How do we deal with these forces of teacher power? And how do we deal with top administrators who are all hung-up in pledges of allegiance to the status quo? There is another whole area here that no one ever wants to deal with in curriculum. I'm talking about middle-management. The big city superintendents swatted out existence like bees buzzing around the honey jar, but middle-management remains. They're like old soldiers, they never die; and they're functioning the same way they did 20 years ago. Anytime you start talking about change, all that they are concerned about are the insecurities. They can't feel all the other forces that surface. How do you deal with and how do you present to a board of education and boards of trustees, a curriculum for a revolutionary age? They will really bomb you on that one.

Arthur W. Foshay

My extension of Dr. Goodlad's remarks will take four aspects. We have to (1) reconceive the goals of schooling, (2) reconceive the nature of the student, (3) reconceive the nature of knowledge (because we are a part of the knowledge

Arthur W. Foshay is a professor at Teachers College, Columbia University.

business), and (4) reconceive what it is to be a teacher. This agenda is required if we are to make intelligent management decisions, as ultimately we must. But I want to stress as heavily as I can that conceiving the problem as a problem of management is simply to slice the bologna in some new way. Management decisions now, in my view, are almost all premature.

What about the new goals for education? Does it mean anything (and I'm sure it does) that 70 per cent of our people are now in large urban centers, and the proportion is going up? Does it mean anything that the population in this country has doubled during my lifetime, so that we are now uncomfortably crowded? It means that we have to find a new version of privacy. We who live in this heavily populated, urbanized land have to find ways of cooperating with one another and of carrying on our interdependent relationships intelligently. We have to find fresh ways of maintaining our individual identities. Each of us is indeed in the midst of a problem of identity, whether or not we fully recognize it.

What should the schools be? If we are to break loose from the "factory" model and stop thinking that we are going to "process" students, we must stop encouraging state legislatures to pass laws about reading methods, which is itself a process arising from the "processing" view of what an education is. If we are going to break out of all that, I would suggest that the function of the schools no longer can be considered to be the development of manpower to fit into the economy or to fit into the society, but rather the *development of legitimate grounds for self-respect.* And I see that, not as a contradiction, but as a flat alternative to the present purpose of the schools as most of us have learned to articulate it.

To do this, we have to allow for three kinds of curricula which operate in the schools and which require official recognition. Curriculum One, which is always in the schools, is the academic curriculum. We do the best we know how with it, and certain important changes in our conception of this curriculum have taken place during the years since 1955. Curriculum Two, sometimes called "the latent curriculum," is the curriculum of social experimentation. We don't explicitly recognize it, but it's always there, as every teacher knows. This curriculum is where students now try to deal with their hang-ups about authority and its nature.

Curriculum Three is the curriculum of individual awareness. Students interrupt themselves and their teachers all the time to talk about their personal development. These conversations are not private, clinical guidance, therapeutic affairs, though they obviously have a therapeutic effect.

Second, we must have a new conception of the student. If the student rebellion means one thing more than any other, it means that students want to take on adult roles earlier. They will not tolerate any longer the prolongation of infancy to 22.

Children are brighter and better educated than ever before, even with all of education's flaws. We have to recognize the fact that they are more aware of what's going on in the world. They are more literate, through the influence of the mass media and through the constant human encounter which goes on in our crowded society. They are much more sophisticated than they used to be, and they say, "An end to infancy!"

I believe that one of the casualties of the next 20 years will be the end of adolescence as we have known it. Look at the roles that the adolescents are taking on now. They are all adult roles—sexual roles, political roles, personal roles. The school of the future will be one that will take these into account, perhaps the way the Parkway School in Philadelphia does, by drawing students directly into the world of work so that they are constantly confronted with reality, with all the warts and hair still on it, not a stylized version of it as in school.

We also need a new conception of knowledge. Young people are saying the cool, objective, disengaged version of the nature of knowledge that we have been proclaiming is simply mistaken. They want it hot, subjective, and engaged. Now, how do we reconcile that with the virtues of rationality? Intellectually, we have to reconcile that aspect of our own nature which is indeed hot, subjective, and engaged (the Id, if you will) with what is cool and objective and logical. And we have not tried to do it. In school we present only half of the equation as if it were the whole thing. So we have to reconceive knowledge. And finally, we have to reconceive what it is to be a teacher. I suggest that we have to decide what it means to say that teaching is an expressive occupation, not an instrumental one. This is sanctimonious talk, and I do not have a better formulation for it than that. The problem for us is to take that slogan and give it some meaning.

139

Reading in the Electronic Age
Jeanne Chall

Reading is full of contradictions and dilemmas. In
many ways it is easy. Indeed, we are rediscovering an old
truth that it can be learned at the mother's knee. Some
children of four or five learn it from an older brother or
sister or even from television commercials. And if the
popular TV series *Sesame Street* is as successful in
teaching pre-reading skills as it appears to be in the
preliminary evaluations, we may have to advance the
reading curriculum in kindergarten and and first grade.

Yet we are now faced with a failure which, according
to former U. S. Commissioner of Education James Allen,
can no longer be tolerated. Too many children of school
age are not learning adequately in spite of, or perhaps
because of, the instruction they receive, and too many
leave school with insufficient reading ability to live
fully.

Jeanne Chall is professor of education at Harvard University.

I will not attempt to analyze here why we have failed. Or even whether we have failed as drastically as is commonly believed. As with all complex phenomena, there is no simple answer. Perhaps if we examine how we have tended to approach the teaching of reading, we may be able to gain some of the perspective needed to cut through the confusion.

But before that, I should like to raise some questions about the necessity of reading itself. In an electronic age, when information and entertainment can be obtained from means other than print, we may well ask whether it is necessary to know how to read. For those children who find it so difficult to learn to read and then to use reading for further learning, perhaps we should concentrate instead on having them learn from films, television, tape recordings, and computers?

This may very well be. In fact, many of the new science and social studies programs such as *Harvard Project Physics* and the Educational Development Corporation's *Man: A Course of Study*[1] make considerable use of films and non-print media. But as far as I know they do not, nor do other such programs, dispense with print entirely. Indeed, my impression is that those programs expressly designed to give each pupil instruction geared to his own style and pace, such as the Individually Prescribed Instruction curriculum of the R and D Center at the University of Pittsburgh, require even more reading than the traditional curricula.

Computer programs that offer perhaps the ultimate in modifying instruction and practice to suit the learner's needs teach primarily in words that have to be read. The student sitting at the computer console must not only read them but also type out his answers. Although it is possible for the illiterate as well as the most highly literate adult to substitute an evening of television viewing for a newspaper, a magazine, or a detective story, both still have to read the road signs as they drive home, grapple with tax forms, and try to figure out leases and installment contracts.

In short, it is quite questionable whether the new media will replace reading in the near future. It is much more probable that as life becomes more complex and specialized, an even higher reading proficiency will be needed. As fewer of us work with our hands and more of us work with our heads, reading skill will be a necessity and a right.

This does not mean that the newer media will not be used more to teach, enrich and entertain. That they are indispensable is captured beautifully in one fifth grader's response to the question of why *Man: A Course of Study* led him to new thinking about man and behavior:

> I think it's partly because there's all the materials like the films, the booklets and, you know, I could keep on going. It makes it more interesting and easier to do instead of: "Here is the book. Read." And you have to give credit to Miss H. She's a great teacher. She made it so that in EDC studies, you look forward, it isn't one big black thing which you don't understand.[2]

His reaction sums up the complementary nature of the various media. And he is even more astute than many technologically bent curriculum developers and planners. He did not forget the teacher as an important variable in the success of the program.

The following finding from the evaluation of the same course makes the interrelationships of the audiovisual media with the more traditional communication skills even more clear:

> The easiest activities for all children were the viewing, listening, talking modes, with the more analytic verbal activities of expressing opinions (as

differentiated from "talk" per se) and doing written work seen as most difficult. Communication skills were viewed by teachers as major growth areas and areas of important change in child behavior over the course of year.[3]

I should like now to turn to the teaching of reading, when it is taught as reading. I will examine two lines of development. For want of more precise terms, I will refer to one as the systematic and to the other as the individualistic.

The two appear at first glance to be polar positions. In fact, one has often been proposed as a way of solving problems that have rightly or wrongly been blamed on the other.

The Systematic Approach

The systematic line of development tends to look at the learning to read process as one that can be analyzed into basic steps that build upon each other. Depending upon the steps that have been postulated, systematic procedures are worked out to give the child instruction and then practice in the various steps—from the simple to the more complex. The steps are then embodied in a package—a published reading program.

These packages are familiar to all of us. The most common format has been a series of graded readers and workbooks for the pupils, and instructional manuals for the teachers.

Some changes have taken place in these programs in the recent past. One has been the tendency to include audio and visual components—some to be used for group instruction and some designed for individual instruction. Indeed, at least one new program is almost predominantly multimedia, with most of its instructional program on films and tapes.

143

There has also been a tendency to produce programs with more limited teaching goals, such as decoding or phonic skills, that can be used in conjunction with more complete programs. Most of these are in the common format of workbooks or duplicatable worksheets. Some have now become more elaborate—using attractive poster-like charts, puppets, and games. Still others come with an audio component and sets of earphones.

For developing comprehension, we still have supplementary sets of graded exercises in paper covered, consumable workbooks. A more recent trend has been to put such exercises on illustrated cards or in small booklets, color-coded by reading level, and organized in a box so that pupils can check their own progress and proceed at their own pace.

Another change incorporated in some of the packages is a programmed learning format, where the tasks are broken down into smaller units and the pupil can, after some instruction from the teacher, proceed more on his own. Although here, too, some checking by the teacher or an aide is needed to assure that learning is taking place.

There have also been some changes recently in the order in which the skills are taught. The reading programs published or revised within the past ten years tend to put an earlier and stronger emphasis on teaching the relationship between sounds and letters.

But the idea of systematization has remained essentially the same—an instructional package (more or less complete) produced by one or more authors—as a way to teach children to read. It is based on the assumption that best results will be achieved when the teacher and the pupils follow the program as it is sequenced by the authors. Of course, the teacher is instructed in the manuals to provide additional practice for those who may not be benefiting as expected. But generally, there is an assumption that all pupils will benefit, even if some proceed slower than others. And for those who fail, other packages have been devised either as alternatives or for remediation.

Systematization has been the predominant way the schools in the United States have approached the teaching of reading. And it seems that this trend is growing even stronger. In fact, the programs are getting ever more elaborate and ever more expensive. A visit to publishers' exhibits at any reading conference makes one wonder whether it isn't perhaps time for someone to rediscover the book, the small book, as an innovative teaching device.

The Individualistic Approach

The individualistic line of development, by way of contrast, tends to assume that learning to read is simple—that it is as natural as learning to speak. Any reasonably healthy child has the desire to learn. He learns best by being exposed to a wide variety of interesting books and by being encouraged to communicate his ideas about them and other things through writing and speaking.

It is therefore assumed that the various reading skills needed to achieve maturity can best be learned as the pupil engages in the reading of books and in writing. If any special instruction is needed, the teacher, another pupil, or some special exercises may serve to supply it. While there is a recognition that pupils proceed through a sequence of tasks of increasing difficulty, there is less concern for a set ordering of these tasks.

Still another assumption is that learning to read is best accomplished on a one-to-one basis. Each child has his own interests and style of learning and putting them all through a packaged program may frustrate some and bore others. The individualistic line of development is probably the one used with children who learn to read before they enter school since it is the simplest for the nonprofessional.

At the present time, it is followed with elementary school pupils by many proponents of what is commonly referred to as Individualized Reading and the Language Experiences approaches to reading—since in theory they do not rely on a published program, but on each child's reading the books he can and wants to read.

Sylvia Ashton Warner's organic method in which she taught each pupil the words that were of interest to him would be another example. John Holt's preference for teaching children by answering their questions about words is another. Still another, with older pupils, is Daniel Feder's prescription in his *Hooked on Books* (1968) where teenagers, retarded in reading and totally lacking in interest, were turned on again by a wealth of paperbacks and magazines.

I could go on with more examples but I am sure the distinction is clear. While the systematic line of development does not discourage the reading of books, and the individualistic does not ignore the teaching of skills, each makes the other's figure its own ground.

As compared to the systematic, the individualistic has the minority position in U. S. schools. In fact two popular schemes for individualization have recently gone the way of systematization. It is now possible to buy an individualized reading program for a particular grade—which includes a set of books, within a span of several levels of difficulty, and already prepared questions and exercises. One can also buy a published set of language-experience materials, which seems almost a contradiction since language-experience implies individuality.

Why am I concerned here with these two lines of development in the teaching of reading—developments that are probably as old as the teaching of reading itself—when my topic is Reading in the Electronic Age? Reading in the Future? It is because I have been troubled lately by the very strong trend toward systematization which, if not tempered sufficiently by the individualistic, may endanger the very purpose for which the systems have been devised. And my impression is that the use of films, tapes, computers, and other technological aids will tend to push us even more in the direction of systematization.

This is not to say that systems are not useful. They have a definite place in the teaching of reading. They can simplify the teacher's task, especially if she is inexperienced or inadequately trained. But they can also complicate her task. Indeed some of the newer programs have become so elaborate that the teacher's time is taken up more in coordinating the different parts and in trying to use them as prescribed than in learning about the children and helping them overcome any difficulties they may have.

There is also a danger in the scientific aura that surrounds most of these programs. The very carefully worked out plans, often produced by an interdisciplinary team of specialists, tend to make the teacher believe that the experts know best. If she is not getting the results that are promised, she often feels that she or the children are at fault, not the program. True, a published reading program in which a publisher may invest as much as $10,000,000 can and should be based on the latest knowledge of how children learn. But that knowledge is quite limited and at best each author gives us only his own interpretation of that knowledge, which may differ considerably from another author's, and from reality.

And what about the pupils? Is reading mainly a matter of answering questions posed by the teacher according to the instructions in the teacher's manuals? Or filling in blanks in workbooks and duplicated worksheets? Is it really different if the questions are asked by the computer and answered on the console typewriter? Of course there is nothing inherent in a reading system that precludes the reading of books just for the fun of it; but, where is the time to come from? And the money?

Some of the systems are so finely programmed that a child who is out ill for a week or two can become quite anxious about catching up on the workbook exercises (and also the computer exercises) he missed. I have found in some of my recent visits to classrooms that this very fine programming is keeping many of the children on material that is much too easy for them. In classroom after classroom I have found that these children can do as well in books or films a reading level or two or even more above what they are working on. Although nothing in the system should prevent skipping parts of programs, this seldom happens for fear that the pupil will not learn some important skill.

There is still another problem that the systems create. Which one should be selected by a school? The promotional materials widely distributed by publishers are not too helpful. They seem to promise everything to everyone and often make one feel that God, motherhood, and country are spurned if their program is not selected. If we look for research evidence of its effectiveness, we are too often disappointed.

What is the solution? One has recently been offered by some publishers—a money-back guarantee. They offer to take back the program or charge a reduced rate if the achieved results are not as good as those promised. Several firms have written performance contracts with school systems to take over the teaching of reading to pupils who are seriously retarded, using their own teachers, a combination of materials and equipment, some of it produced by the firm, some by others. The contract also calls for training some teachers and supervisors in the school system. Incentives have been worked out for pupils who improve their skill, and for teachers whose pupils achieve good results. Payment by the school is based on measured results, with full payment expected only if pupils make the agreed-upon progress, and rates reduced proportionate to whatever progress is made. Whether this is a viable solution is yet to be determined.

Another solution recommended by the National Advisory Committee on Dyslexia and Related Reading Disorders (1969)[4] is that some agency in the Department of Health, Education and Welfare be set up to run continuous evaluations of instructional materials and procedures to be disseminated to the schools—similar to a pure food and drug administration.

I wonder, though, whether we cannot expect the publishers to take on some of the responsibility for evaluating their own programs. It seems to me that they have a responsibility for giving some viable proof of effectiveness. Even though some may offer schools a money-back guarantee, pupil time and teacher time are big investments that are difficult to evaluate in monetary terms.

Although I have gone into considerable detail about the dangers of systematization, I must make clear that I am not opposed to systems; nor, do I think we can achieve better results by turning solely to the individualistic. In order to succeed with the individualistic requires even a greater knowledge of pupils, books, and children on the part of the teacher. It takes more knowledge of reading on the part of the teacher to make a suggestion here and another there. It takes organizational ability which all teachers do not have. Therefore it will take more thorough training of teachers by colleges and universities and higher standards of certifying teachers of reading by state departments of education.

And yet if the various reading programs and systems continue in the direction of the ever more elaborate, ever more expensive, and ever more time-consuming, I fear we may be preparing ourselves for a strong reaction. Before this comes it is well to ask ourselves the simple questions: Is all this necessary? Is it as difficult as all that? We may find that a book, a blackboard, a piece of chalk, and a knowledgeable and sympathetic adult may do some of it just as well.

NOTES

1. Janet P. Hanley, Dean K. Whitla et al., *An Evaluation of Man: A Course of Study*, 2 Vols. (Cambridge, Mass.: Educational Development Corp., 1970).
2. *Ibid.*
3. *Ibid.*
4. *Reading Disorders in the United States*, Report of the Secretary's National Advisory Committee on Dyslexia and Related Reading Disorders, HEW, Washington, D. C., 1969.

DATE DUE

June